THE FUNCTION OF THE POET
AND OTHER ESSAYS

THE
FUNCTION OF THE POET

AND OTHER ESSAYS

BY JAMES RUSSELL LOWELL, *1819 - 1891*

COLLECTED AND EDITED BY
ALBERT MORDELL

KENNIKAT PRESS, INC./PORT WASHINGTON, N. Y.

THE FUNCTION OF THE POET

Copyright 1920 by Houghton Mifflin Company
Reissued in 1967 by Kennikat Press
Library of Congress Catalog Card No: 67-27621

Manufactured in the United States of America

ESSAY AND GENERAL LITERATURE INDEX REPRINT SERIES

PREFACE

THE Centenary Celebration of James Russell Lowell last year showed that he has become more esteemed as a critic and essayist than as a poet. Lowell himself felt that his true calling was in critical work rather than in poetry, and he wrote very little verse in the latter part of his life. He was somewhat chagrined that the poetic flame of his youth did not continue to glow, but he resigned himself to his fate; nevertheless, it should be remembered that "The Vision of Sir Launfal," "The Biglow Papers," and "The Commemoration Ode" are enough to make the reputation of any poet.

The present volume sustains Lowell's right to be considered one of the great American critics. The literary merit of some of the essays herein is in many respects nowise inferior to that in some of the volumes he collected himself. The articles are all exquisitely and carefully written, and the style of even the book reviews displays that quality found in his best writings which Ferris Greenslet has appropriately described as "savory." That such a quantity of good literature by so able a writer as Lowell should have been allowed to repose buried in the files of old magazines so long is rather unfortunate. The fact that

Lowell did not collect them is a tribute to his modesty, a tribute all the more worthy in these days when some writers of ephemeral reviews on ephemeral books think it their duty to collect their opinions in book form.

The essays herein represent the matured author as they were written in the latter part of his life, between his thirty-sixth and fifty-seventh years. The only early essay is the one on Poe. It appeared in *Graham's Magazine* for February, 1845, and was reprinted by Griswold in his edition of Poe. It has also been reprinted in later editions of Poe, but has never been included in any of Lowell's works. This was no doubt due to the slight break in the relations between Poe and Lowell, due to Poe's usual accusations of plagiarism. The essay still remains one of the best on Poe ever written.

Though Lowell became in later life quite conservative and academic, it should not be thought that these essays show no sympathy with liberal ideas. He was also appreciative of the first works of new writers, and had good and prophetic insight. His favorable reviews of the first works of Howells and James, and the subsequent career of these two men, indicate the sureness of Lowell's critical mind. Many readers will enjoy, in these days of the ouija board and messages from the dead, the raps at spiritualism here and there. Moreover, there is a passage in the

PREFACE

first essay showing that Lowell, before Freud, understood the psychoanalytic theory of genius in its connection with childhood memories. The passage follows Lowell's narration of the story of little Montague.

None of the essays in this volume has appeared in book form except a few fragments from some of the opening five essays which were reported from Lowell's lectures in the *Boston Advertiser*, in 1855, and were privately printed some years ago. Charles Eliot Norton performed a service to the world when he published in the *Century Magazine* in 1893 and 1894 some lectures from Lowell's manuscripts. These lectures are now collected and form the first five essays in this book. I have also retained Professor Norton's introductions and notes. Attention is called to his remark that "The Function of the Poet" is not unworthy to stand with Sidney's and Shelley's essays on poetry.

The rest of the essays in this volume appeared in Lowell's lifetime in the *Atlantic Monthly*, the *North American Review*, and the *Nation*. They were all anonymous, but are assigned to Lowell by George Willis Cooke in his "Bibliography of James Russell Lowell." Lowell was editor of the *Atlantic* from the time of its founding in 1857 to May, 1861. He was editor of the *North American Review* from January, 1864, to the time he left for Europe in 1872. With one exception (that on "Poetry and Nationalism" which formed the greater part of a review of the poems of Howells's friend Piatt), all the articles from these two magazines, reprinted in this volume, appeared during Lowell's editorship. These articles include reviews of poems by his friends Longfellow and Whittier. And in his review of "The Courtship of Miles Standish," Lowell makes effective use of his scholarship to introduce a lengthy and interesting discourse on the dactylic hexameter.

While we are on the subject of the New England poets a word about the present misunderstanding and tendency to underrate thèm may not be out of place. Because it is growing to be the consensus of opinion that the two greatest poets America has produced are Whitman and Poe, it does not follow that the New-Englanders must be relegated to the scrap-heap. Nor do I see any inconsistency in a man whose taste permits him to enjoy both the free verse and unpuritanic (if I may coin a word) poems of Masters and Sandburg, and also Whittier's "Snow-Bound" and Longfellow's "Courtship of Miles Standish." Though these poems are not profound, there is something of the universal in them. They have pleasant school-day memories for all of us and will no doubt have such for our children.

Lowell's cosmopolitan tastes may be seen in his essays on men so different as Thackeray, Swift, and

Plutarch. Hardly any one knows that he even wrote about these authors. Lowell preferred Thackeray to Dickens, a judgment in which many people to-day no longer agree with him. As a young man he hated Swift, but he gives us a sane study of him. The review of Plutarch's "Essays" edited by Goodwin, with an introduction by Emerson, is also of interest.

The last essay in the volume on "A Plea for Freedom from Speech and Figures of Speech-Makers" shows Lowell's satirical powers at their best. Ferris Greenslet tells us, in his book on Lowell, that the Philip Vandal whose eloquence Lowell ridicules is Wendell Phillips. The essay gives Lowell's humorous comments on various matters, especially on contemporary types of orators, reformers, and heroes. It represents Lowell as he is most known to us, the Lowell who is always ready with fun and who set the world agog with his "Biglow Papers."

Lowell's work as a critic dates from the rare volume "Conversations on Some of the Old Poets," published in 1844 in his twenty-fifth year, includes his best-known volumes "Among My Books" and "My Study Windows," and most fitly concludes with the "Latest Literary Essays," published in the year of his death in 1891. My sincere hope is that this book will not be found to be an unworthy successor to these volumes.

Though some of Lowell's literary opinions are old-fashioned to us (one author even wrote an entire volume to demolish Lowell's reputation as a critic), there is much in his work that the world will not let die. He is highly regarded abroad, and he is one of the few men in our literature who produced creative criticism.

Thanks and acknowledgments are due the *Century Magazine* and the literary representatives of Lowell, for permission to reprint in this volume the first five essays, which are copyrighted and were published in the *Century Magazine*.

ALBERT MORDELL

Philadelphia, January 13, 1920

CONTENTS

ON POETRY AND BELLES-LETTRES

REVIEWS OF CONTEMPORARIES

CONTENTS

TWO GREAT AUTHORS

ON POETRY AND BELLES-LETTRES

THE FUNCTION OF THE POET

THIS was the concluding lecture in the course which Lowell read before the Lowell Institute in the winter of 1855. Doubtless Lowell never printed it because, as his genius matured, he felt that its assertions were too absolute, and that its style bore too many marks of haste in composition, and was too rhetorical for an essay to be read in print. How rapid was the growth of his intellectual judgment, and the broadening of his imaginative view, may be seen by comparing it with his essays on Swinburne, on Percival, and on Rousseau, published in 1866 and 1867 — essays in which the topics of this lecture were touched upon anew, though not treated at large.

But the spirit of this lecture is so fine, its tone so full of the enthusiasm of youth, its conception of the poet so lofty, and the truths it contains so important, that it may well be prized as the expression of a genius which, if not yet mature, is already powerful, and aquiline alike in vision and in sweep of wing. It is not unworthy to stand with Sidney's and with Shelley's "Defence of Poesy," and it is fitted to warm and inspire the poetic heart of the youth of this generation, no less than of that to which it was first addressed. As a close to the lecture Lowell read his beautiful (then unpublished) poem "To the Muse."

Charles Eliot Norton

WHETHER, as some philosophers assume, we possess only the fragments of a great cycle of knowledge in whose centre stood the primeval man in friendly relation with the powers of the universe, and build our hovels out of the ruins of our ancestral palace; or whether, according to the development theory of others, we are rising gradually, and have come up out of an atom instead of descending from an Adam, so that the proudest pedigree might run up to a barnacle or a zoöphyte at last, are questions that will keep for a good many centuries yet. Confining myself to what little we can learn from history, we find tribes rising slowly out of barbarism to a higher or lower point of culture and civility, and everywhere the poet also is found, under one name or other, changing in certain outward respects, but essentially the same.

And however far we go back, we shall find this also — that the poet and the priest were united originally in the same person; which means that the poet was he who was conscious of the world of spirit as well as that of sense, and was the ambassador of the gods to men. This was his highest function, and hence his name of "seer." He was the discoverer and declarer of the perennial beneath the deciduous. His were the *epea pteroenta*, the true "winged words" that could fly down the unexplored future and carry the names of ancestral heroes, of the brave and wise and good. It was thus that the poet could reward virtue, and, by and by, as society grew more complex, could burn in the brand of shame. This is Homer's character of Demodocus, in the eighth book of the "Odyssey," "whom the Muse loved and gave the good and ill" — the gift of conferring good or evil immortality. The first histories were in verse; and sung as they were at feasts and gatherings of the people, they awoke in men the desire of fame, which is the first promoter of courage and self-trust, because it teaches men by degrees to appeal from the present to the future. We may fancy what the influence of the early epics was when they were recited to men who claimed the heroes celebrated in them for their ancestors, by what Bouchardon, the sculptor, said, only two centuries ago: "When I read Homer, I feel as if I were twenty feet high." Nor have poets lost their power over the future in modern times. Dante lifts up by the hair the face of some petty traitor, the Smith or Brown of some provincial Italian town, lets the fire of his Inferno glare upon it for a moment, and it is printed forever on the memory of mankind. The historians may iron out the shoulders of Richard the Third as smooth as they can, they will never get over the wrench that Shakespeare gave them.

The peculiarity of almost all early literature is that it seems to have a double meaning, that, underneath its natural, we find ourselves continually seeing or suspecting a supernatural meaning. In the older epics the characters seem to be half typical and only half historical. Thus did the early poets endeavor to make realities out of appearances; for, except a few typical men in whom certain ideas get embodied, the generations of mankind are mere apparitions who come out of the dark for a purposeless moment, and reënter the dark again after they have performed the nothing they came for.

Gradually, however, the poet as the "seer" became secondary to the "maker." His office became that of entertainer rather than teacher. But always something of the old tradition was kept alive. And if he has now come to be looked upon merely as the best expresser, the gift of seeing is implied as necessarily antecedent to that, and of seeing very deep, too. If any man would seem to have written without any conscious moral, that man is Shakespeare. But that must be a dull sense, indeed, which does not see through his tragic — yes, and his comic — masks awful eyes that flame with something intenser and deeper than a mere scenic meaning — a meaning out of the great deep that is behind and beyond all human and merely personal character. Nor was Shakespeare himself unconscious of his place as a teacher and profound moralist: witness that sonnet in which he bewails his having neglected sometimes the errand that was laid upon him:

> Alas, 't is true I have gone here and there,
> And made myself a motley to the view,
> Gored mine own thoughts, sold cheap what is most dear,
> Made old offences of affections new;
> Most true it is that I have look'd on truth
> Askance and strangely;

the application of which is made clear by the next sonnet, in which he distinctly alludes to his profession.

THE FUNCTION OF THE POET

There is this unmistakable stamp on all the great poets — that, however in little things they may fall below themselves, whenever there comes a great and noble thing to say, they say it greatly and nobly, and bear themselves most easily in the royalties of thought and language. There is not a mature play of Shakespeare's in which great ideas do not jut up in mountainous permanence, marking forever the boundary of provinces of thought, and known afar to many kindreds of men.

And it is for this kind of sight, which we call insight, and not for any faculty of observation and description, that we value the poet. It is in proportion as he has this that he is an adequate expresser, and not a juggler with words. It is by means of this that for every generation of man he plays the part of "namer." Before him, as before Adam, the creation passes to be named anew: first the material world; then the world of passions and emotions; then the world of ideas. But whenever a great imagination comes, however it may delight itself with imaging the outward beauty of things, however it may seem to flow thoughtlessly away in music like a brook, yet the shadow of heaven lies also in its depth beneath the shadow of earth. Continually the visible universe suggests the invisible. We are forever feeling this in Shakespeare. His imagination went down to the very bases of things, and while his characters are the most natural that poet ever created, they are also perfectly ideal, and are more truly the personifications of abstract thoughts and passions than those of any allegorical writer whatever.

Even in what seems so purely a picturesque poem as the "Iliad," we feel something of this. Beholding as Homer did, from the tower of contemplation, the eternal mutability and nothing permanent but change, he must look underneath the show for the reality. Great captains and conquerors came forth out of the eternal silence, entered it again with their trampling hosts, and shoutings, and trumpet-blasts, and were as utterly gone as those echoes of their deeds which he sang, and which faded with the last sound of his voice and the last tremble of his lyre. History relating outward events alone was an unmeaning gossip, with the world for a village. This life could only become other than phantasmagoric, could only become real, as it stood related to something that was higher and permanent. Hence the idea of Fate, of a higher power unseen — that shadow, as of an eagle circling to its swoop, which flits stealthily and swiftly across the windy plains of Troy. In the "Odyssey" we find pure allegory.

Now, under all these names — praiser, seer, soothsayer — we find the same idea lurking. The poet is he who can best see and best say what is ideal — what belongs to the world of soul and of beauty. Whether he celebrate the brave and good man, or the gods, or the beautiful as it appears in man or nature, something of a religious character still clings to him; he is the revealer of Deity. He may be unconscious of his mission; he may be false to it; but in proportion as he is a great poet, he rises to the level of it the more often. He does not always directly rebuke what is bad and base, but indirectly by making us feel what delight there is in the good and fair. If he besiege evil, it is with such beautiful engines of war (as Plutarch tells us of Demetrius) that the besieged themselves are charmed with them. Whoever reads the great poets cannot but be made better by it, for they always introduce him to a higher society, to a greater style of manners and of thinking. Whoever learns to love what is beautiful is made incapable of the low and mean and bad. If Plato excludes the poets from his Republic, it is expressly on the ground that they speak unworthy things of the gods; that is, that they have lost the secret of their art, and use artificial types instead of speaking the true universal language of imagination. He who translates the divine into the vulgar, the spiritual into the sensual, is the reverse of a poet.

The poet, under whatever name, always stands for the same thing — imagination. And imagination in its highest form gives him the power, as it were, of assuming the consciousness of whatever he speaks

about, whether man or beast, or rock or tree. It is the
ring of Canace, which whoso has on understands the
language of all created things. And as regards expression, it seems to enable the poet to condense the
whole of himself into a single word. Therefore, when
a great poet has said a thing, it is finally and utterly
expressed, and has as many meanings as there are
men who read his verse. A great poet is something
more than an interpreter between man and nature;
he is also an interpreter between man and his own
nature. It is he who gives us those key-words, the
possession of which makes us masters of all the un-
suspected treasure-caverns of thought, and feeling,
and beauty which open under the dusty path of our
daily life.

And it is not merely a dry lexicon that he compiles,
— a thing which enables us to translate from one
dead dialect into another as dead, — but all his verse
is instinct with music, and his words open windows
on every side to pictures of scenery and life. The difference between the dry fact and the poem is as great
as that between reading the shipping news and seeing
the actual coming and going of the crowd of stately
ships, — "the city on the inconstant billows danc-
ing," — as there is between ten minutes of happiness
and ten minutes by the clock. Everybody remembers
the story of the little Montague who was stolen and
sold to the chimney-sweep: how he could dimly re-

member lying in a beautiful chamber; how he carried with him in all his drudgery the vision of a fair, sad mother's face that sought him everywhere in vain; how he threw himself one day, all sooty as he was from his toil, on a rich bed and fell asleep, and how a kind person woke him, questioned him, pieced together his broken recollections for him, and so at last made the visions of the beautiful chamber and the fair, sad countenance real to him again. It seems to me that the offices that the poet does for us are typified in this nursery-tale. We all of us have our vague reminiscences of the stately home of our childhood, — for we are all of us poets and geniuses in our youth, while earth is all new to us, and the chalice of every buttercup is brimming with the wine of poesy, — and we all remember the beautiful, motherly countenance which nature bent over us there. But somehow we all get stolen away thence; life becomes to us a sooty taskmaster, and we crawl through dark passages without end — till suddenly the word of some poet redeems us, makes us know who we are, and of helpless orphans makes us the heir to a great estate. It is to our true relations with the two great worlds of outward and inward nature that the poet reintroduces us.

But the imagination has a deeper use than merely to give poets a power of expression. It is the everlasting preserver of the world from blank materialism.

It forever puts matter in the wrong, and compels it to show its title to existence. Wordsworth tells us that in his youth he was sometimes obliged to touch the walls to find if they were visionary or no, and such experiences are not uncommon with persons who converse much with their own thoughts. Dr. Johnson said that to kick one's foot against a stone was a sufficient confutation of Berkeley, and poor old Pyrrho has passed into a proverb because, denying the objectivity of matter, he was run over by a cart and killed. But all that he affirmed was that to the soul the cart was no more real than its own imaginative reproduction of it, and perhaps the shade of the philosopher ran up to the first of his deriders who crossed the Styx with a triumphant "I told you so! The cart did not run over *me*, for here I am without a bone broken."

And, in another sense also, do those poets who deal with human character, as all the greater do, continually suggest to us the purely phantasmal nature of life except as it is related to the world of ideas. For are not their personages more real than most of those in history? Is not Lear more authentic and permanent than Lord Raglan? Their realm is a purely spiritual one in which space and time and costume are nothing. What matters it that Shakespeare puts a seaport in Bohemia, and knew less geography than Tommy who goes to the district school? He understood eternal boundaries, such as are laid down on no chart, and are not defined by such transitory affairs as mountain chains, rivers, and seas.

No great movement of the human mind takes place without the concurrent beat of those two wings, the imagination and the understanding. It is by the understanding that we are enabled to make the most of this world, and to use the collected material of experience in its condensed form of practical wisdom; and it is the imagination which forever beckons toward that other world which is always future, and makes us discontented with this. The one rests upon experience; the other leans forward and listens after the *in*experienced, and shapes the features of that future with which it is forever in travail. The imagination might be defined as the common sense of the invisible world, as the understanding is of the visible; and as those are the finest individual characters in which the two moderate and rectify each other, so those are the finest eras where the same may be said of society. In the voyage of life, not only do we depend on the needle, true to its earthly instincts, but upon observation of the fixed stars, those beacons lighted upon the eternal promontories of heaven above the stirs and shiftings of our lower system.

But it seems to be thought that we have come upon the earth too late, that there has been a feast of imagination formerly, and all that is left for us is to steal

the scraps. We hear that there is no poetry in railroads and steamboats and telegraphs, and especially
none in Brother Jonathan. If this be true, so much
the worse for him. But because *he* is a materialist,
shall there be no more poets? When we have said that
we live in a materialistic age we have said something
which meant more than we intended. If we say it in
the way of blame, we have said a foolish thing, for
probably one age is as good as another, and, at any
rate, the worst is good enough company for us. The
age of Shakespeare was richer than our own, only because it was lucky enough to have such a pair of eyes
as his to see it, and such a gift of speech as his to report it. And so there is always room and occasion for
the poet, who continues to be, just as he was in the
early time, nothing more nor less than a "seer." He
is always the man who is willing to take the age he
lives in on trust, as the very best that ever was.
Shakespeare did not sit down and cry for the water of
Helicon to turn the wheels of his little private mill
at the Bankside. He appears to have gone more
quietly about his business than any other playwright
in London, to have drawn off what water-power he
needed from the great prosy current of affairs that
flows alike for all and in spite of all, to have ground
for the public what grist they wanted, coarse or fine,
and it seems a mere piece of luck that the smooth
stream of his activity reflected with such ravishing

clearness every changing mood of heaven and earth, every stick and stone, every dog and clown and courtier that stood upon its brink. It is a curious illustration of the friendly manner in which Shakespeare received everything that came along, — of what a *present* man he was, — that in the very same year that the mulberry-tree was brought into England, he got one and planted it in his garden at Stratford.

It is perfectly true that this is a materialistic age, and for that very reason we want our poets all the more. We find that every generation contrives to catch its singing larks without the sky's falling. When the poet comes, he always turns out to be the man who discovers that the passing moment is the inspired one, and that the secret of poetry is not to have lived in Homer's day, or Dante's, but to be alive now. To be alive now, that is the great art and mystery. They are dead men who live in the past, and men yet unborn that live in the future. We are like Hans in Luck, forever exchanging the burdensome good we have for something else, till at last we come home empty-handed.

That pale-faced drudge of Time opposite me there, that weariless sexton whose callous hands bury our rosy hours in the irrevocable past, is even now reaching forward to a moment as rich in life, in character, and thought, as full of opportunity, as any since Adam. This little isthmus that we are now standing on is the point to which martyrs in their triumphant pain, prophets in their fervor, and poets in their ecstasy, looked forward as the golden future, as the land too good for them to behold with mortal eyes; it is the point toward which the faint-hearted and desponding hereafter will look back as the priceless past when there was still some good and virtue and opportunity left in the world.

The people who feel their own age prosaic are those who see only its costume. And that is what makes it prosaic — that we have not faith enough in ourselves to think our own clothes good enough to be presented to posterity in. The artists fancy that the court dress of posterity is that of Van Dyck's time, or Cæsar's. I have seen the model of a statue of Sir Robert Peel, — a statesman whose merit consisted in yielding gracefully to the present, — in which the sculptor had done his best to travesty the real man into a make-believe Roman. At the period when England produced its greatest poets, we find exactly the reverse of this, and we are thankful that the man who made the monument of Lord Bacon had genius to copy every button of his dress, everything down to the rosettes on his shoes, and then to write under his statue, "Thus sat Francis Bacon" — not "Cneius Pompeius" — "Viscount Verulam." Those men had faith even in their own shoe-strings.

After all, how is our poor scapegoat of a nineteenth

century to blame? Why, for not being the seventeenth, to be sure! It is always raining opportunity, but it seems it was only the men two hundred years ago who were intelligent enough not to hold their cups bottom-up. We are like beggars who think if a piece of gold drop into their palm it must be counterfeit, and would rather change it for the smooth-worn piece of familiar copper. And so, as we stand in our mendicancy by the wayside, Time tosses carefully the great golden to-day into our hats, and we turn it over grumblingly and suspiciously, and are pleasantly surprised at finding that we can exchange it for beef and potatoes. Till Dante's time the Italian poets thought no language good enough to put their nothings into but Latin, — and indeed a dead tongue was the best for dead thoughts, — but Dante found the common speech of Florence, in which men bargained and scolded and made love, good enough for him, and out of the world around him made a poem such as no Roman ever sang.

In our day, it is said despairingly, the understanding reigns triumphant: it is the age of common sense. If this be so, the wisest way would be to accept it manfully. But, after all, what is the meaning of it? Looking at the matter superficially, one would say that a striking difference between our science and that of the world's gray fathers is that there is every day less and less of the element of wonder in it. What they saw written in light upon the great arch of heaven, and, by a magnificent reach of sympathy, of which we are incapable, associated with the fall of monarchs and the fate of man, is for us only a professor, a piece of chalk, and a blackboard. The solemn and unapproachable skies we have vulgarized; we have peeped and botanized among the flowers of light, pulled off every petal, fumbled in every calyx, and reduced them to the bare stem of order and class. The stars can no longer maintain their divine reserves, but whenever there is a conjunction and congress of planets, every enterprising newspaper sends thither its special reporter with his telescope. Over those arcana of life where once a mysterious presence brooded, we behold scientific explorers skipping like so many incarnate notes of interrogation. We pry into the counsels of the great powers of nature, we keep our ears at the keyhole, and know everything that is going to happen. There is no longer any sacred inaccessibility, no longer any enchanting unexpectedness, and life turns to prose the moment there is nothing unattainable. It needs no more a voice out of the unknown proclaiming "Great Pan is dead!" We have found his tombstone, deciphered the arrow-headed inscription upon it, know his age to a day, and that he died universally regretted.

Formerly science was poetry. A mythology which broods over us in our cradle, which mingles with the lullaby of the nurse, which peoples the day with the possibility of divine encounters, and night with intimation of demonic ambushes, is something quite other, as the material for thought and poetry, from one that we take down from our bookshelves, as sapless as the shelf it stood on, as remote from all present sympathy with man or nature as a town history with its genealogies of Mr. Nobody's great-grandparents.

We have utilized everything. The Egyptians found a hint of the solar system in the concentric circles of the onion, and revered it as a symbol, while we respect it as a condiment in cookery, and can pass through all Weathersfield without a thought of the stars. Our world is a museum of natural history; that of our forefathers was a museum of supernatural history. And the rapidity with which the change has been going on is almost startling, when we consider that so modern and historical a personage as Queen Elizabeth was reigning at the time of the death of Dr. John Faustus, out of whose story the Teutonic imagination built up a mythus that may be set beside that of Prometheus.

Science, looked at scientifically, is bare and bleak enough. On those sublime heights the air is too thin for the lungs, and blinds the eyes. It is much better living down in the valleys, where one cannot see farther than the next farmhouse. Faith was never found in the bottom of a crucible, nor peace arrived at by analysis or synthesis. But all this is because science has become too grimly intellectual, has divorced itself from the moral and imaginative part of man. Our results are not arrived at in that spirit which led Kepler (who had his theory-traps set all along the tracks of the stars to catch a discovery) to say, "In my opinion the occasions of new discoveries have been no less wonderful than the discoveries themselves."

But we are led back continually to the fact that science cannot, if it would, disengage itself from human nature and from imagination. No two men have ever argued together without at least agreeing in this, that something more than proof is required to produce conviction, and that a logic which is capable of grinding the stubbornest facts to powder (as every man's *own* logic always is) is powerless against so delicate a structure as the brain. Do what we will, we cannot contrive to bring together the yawning edges of proof and belief, to weld them into one. When Thor strikes Skrymir with his terrible hammer, the giant asks if a leaf has fallen. I need not appeal to the Thors of argument in the pulpit, the senate, and the mass-meeting, if they have not sometimes found the popular giant as provokingly insensible. The $\sqrt{-x}$ is nothing in comparison with the chance-caught smell of a single flower which by the magic of association recreates for us the unquestioning day of childhood. Demonstration may lead to the very gate of heaven, but there she makes us a civil bow, and leaves us to make our way back again to Faith, who has the key. That science which is of the intellect alone steps with indifferent foot upon the dead body of Belief, if only she may reach higher or see farther.

But we cannot get rid of our wonder — we who have brought down the wild lightning, from writing fiery doom upon the walls of heaven, to be our errand-boy and penny-postman. Wonder is crude imagination; and it is necessary to us, for man shall not live by bread alone, and exact knowledge is not enough. Do we get nearer the truth or farther from it that we have got a gas or an imponderable fluid instead of a spirit? We go on exorcising one thing after another, but what boots it? The evasive genius flits into something else, and defies us. The powers of the outer and inner world form hand in hand a magnetic circle for whose connection man is necessary. It is the imagination that takes his hand and clasps it with that other stretched to him in the dark, and for which he was vainly groping. It is that which renews the mystery in nature, makes it wonderful and beautiful again, and out of the gases of the man of science remakes the old spirit. But we seem to have created too many wonders to be capable of wondering any longer; as Coleridge said, when asked if he believed in ghosts, that he had seen too many of them. But nature all the more imperatively demands it, and science can at best but scotch it, not kill it. In this day of newspapers and electric telegraphs, in which common sense and ridicule can magnetize a whole continent between dinner and tea, we say that such a phenomenon as Mahomet were impossible, and behold Joe Smith and the State of Deseret! Turning over the yellow leaves of the same copy of "Webster on Witchcraft" which Cotton Mather studied, I thought, "Well, that goblin is laid at last!" — and while I mused the tables were turning, and the chairs beating the devil's tattoo all over Christendom. I have a neighbor who dug down through tough strata of clay to a spring pointed out by a witch-hazel rod in the hands of a seventh son's seventh son, and the water is the sweeter to him for the wonder that is mixed with it. After all, it seems that our scientific gas, be it never so brilliant, is not equal to the dingy old Aladdin's lamp.

It is impossible for men to live in the world without poetry of some sort or other. If they cannot get the best they will get some substitute for it, and thus seem to verify Saint Augustine's slur that it is wine of devils. The mind bound down too closely to what is practical either becomes inert, or revenges itself by rushing into the savage wilderness of "isms." The insincerity of our civilization has disgusted some persons so much that they have sought refuge in Indian wigwams and found refreshment in taking a scalp now and then. Nature insists above all things upon balance. She contrives to maintain a harmony between the material and spiritual, nor allows the cerebrum an expansion at the cost of the cerebellum. If the character, for example, run on one side into religious enthusiasm, it is not unlikely to develop on the other a counterpoise of worldly prudence. Thus the Shaker and the Moravian are noted for thrift, and mystics are not always the worst managers. Through all changes of condition and experience man continues to be a citizen of the world of idea as well as the world of fact, and the tax-gatherers of both are punctual.

And these antitheses which we meet with in individual character we cannot help seeing on the larger stage of the world also, a moral accompanying a material development. History, the great satirist, brings together Alexander and the blower of peas to hint to us that the tube of the one and the sword of the other were equally transitory; but meanwhile Aristotle was conquering kingdoms out of the unknown, and establishing a dynasty of thought from whose hand the sceptre has not yet passed. So there are Charles V, and Luther; the expansion of trade resulting from the Spanish and Portuguese discoveries, and the Elizabethan literature; the Puritans seeking spiritual El Dorados while so much valor and thought were spent in finding mineral ones. It seems to be the purpose of God that a certain amount of genius shall go to each generation, particular quantities being represented by individuals, and while no *one* is complete in himself, all collectively make up a whole ideal figure of a man. Nature is not like certain varieties of the apple that cannot bear two years in succession. It is only that her expansions are uniform in all directions, that in every age she completes her circle, and like a tree adds a ring to her growth be it thinner or thicker.

Every man is conscious that he leads two lives, the one trivial and ordinary, the other sacred and recluse; the one which he carries to the dinner-table and to his daily work, which grows old with his body and dies with it, the other that which is made up of the few inspiring moments of his higher aspiration and attainment, and in which his youth survives for him, his dreams, his unquenchable longings for something nobler than success. It is this life which the poets nourish for him, and sustain with their immortalizing nectar. Through them he feels once more the white innocence of his youth. His faith in something nobler than gold and iron and cotton comes back to him, not as an upbraiding ghost that wrings its pale hands and is gone, but beautiful and inspiring as a first love that recognizes nothing in him that is not high and noble. The poets are nature's perpetual pleaders, and protest with us against what is worldly. Out of their own undying youth they speak to ours. "Wretched is the man," says Goethe, "who has learned to despise the dreams of his youth!" It is from this misery that the imagination and the poets, who are its spokesmen, rescue us. The world goes to church, kneels to the eternal Purity, and then contrives to sneer at innocence and ignorance of evil by calling it green. Let every man thank God for what little there may be left in him of his vernal sweetness. Let him thank God if he have still the capacity for feeling an unmarketable enthusiasm, for that will make him worthy of the society of the noble dead, of the companionship of the poets. And let him love the poets for keeping youth young, woman womanly, and beauty beautiful.

There is as much poetry as ever in the world if we only knew how to find it out; and as much imagination, perhaps, only that it takes a more prosaic direction. Every man who meets with misfortune, who is stripped of material prosperity, finds that he has a little outlying mountain-farm of imagination, which did not appear in the schedule of his effects, on which his spirit is able to keep itself alive, though he never thought of it while he was fortunate. Job turns out to be a great poet as soon as his flocks and herds are taken away from him.

There is no reason why our continent should not sing as well as the rest. We have had the practical forced upon us by our position. We have had a whole hemisphere to clear up and put to rights. And we are descended from men who were hardened and stiffened by a downright wrestle with necessity. There was no chance for poetry among the Puritans. And yet if any people have a right to imagination, it should be the descendants of these very Puritans. They had enough of it, or they could never have conceived the great epic they did, whose books are States, and which is written on this continent from Maine to California.

But there seems to be another reason why we should not become a poetical people. Formerly the poet embodied the hopes and desires of men in visible types. He gave them the shoes of swiftness, the cap of invisibility and the purse of Fortunatus. These were once stories for grown men, and not for the nursery as now. We are apt ignorantly to wonder how our forefathers could find satisfaction in fiction the absurdity of which any of our primary-school children could demonstrate. But we forget that the world's gray fathers were children themselves, and that in their little world, with its circle of the black unknown all about it, the imagination was as active as it is with people in the dark. Look at a child's toys, and we shall understand the matter well enough. Imagination is the fairy godmother (every child has one still), at the wave of whose wand sticks become heroes, the closet in which she has been shut fifty times for being naughty is turned into a palace, and a bit of lath acquires all the potency of Excalibur.

But nowadays it is the understanding itself that has turned poet. In her railroads she has given us the shoes of swiftness. Fine-Ear herself could not hear so far as she, who in her magnetic telegraph can listen in Boston and hear what is going on in New Orleans. And what need of Aladdin's lamp when a man can build a palace with a patent pill? The office of the poet seems to be reversed, and he must give back these miracles of the understanding to poetry again, and find out what there is imaginative in steam and iron and telegraph-wires. After all, there is as much poetry in the iron horses that eat fire as in those of Diomed that fed on men. If you cut an apple across you may trace in it the lines of the blossom that the bee hummed around in May, and so the soul of poetry survives in things prosaic. Borrowing money on a bond does not seem the most promising subject in the world, but Shakespeare found the "Merchant of Venice" in it. Themes of song are waiting everywhere for the right man to sing them, like those enchanted swords which no one can pull out of the rock till the hero comes, and he finds no more trouble than in plucking a violet.

John Quincy Adams, making a speech at New Bedford, many years ago, reckoned the number of whaleships (if I remember rightly) that sailed out of that port, and, comparing it with some former period, took it as a type of American success. But, alas! it is with quite other oil that those far-shining lamps of a nation's true glory which burn forever must be filled. It is not by any amount of material splendor or prosperity, but only by moral greatness, by ideas, by works of imagination, that a race can conquer the future. No voice comes to us from the once mighty Assyria but the hoot of the owl that nests amid her crumbling palaces. Of Carthage, whose merchant-fleets once furled their sails in every port of the known world, nothing is left but the deeds of Hannibal. She lies dead on the shore of her once subject sea, and the wind of the desert only flings its handfuls of burial-sand upon her corpse. A fog can blot Holland or Switzerland out of existence. But how large is the space occupied in the maps of the soul by little Athens and powerless Italy! They were great by the soul, and their vital force is as indestructible as the soul.

Till America has learned to love art, not as an amusement, not as the mere ornament of her cities, not as a superstition of what is *comme il faut* for a great nation, but for its humanizing and ennobling energy, for its power of making men better by arousing in them a perception of their own instincts for what is beautiful, and therefore sacred and religious, and an eternal rebuke of the base and worldly, she will not have succeeded in that high sense which alone makes a nation out of a people, and raises it from a dead name to a living power. Were our little mother-island sunk beneath the sea, or, worse, were she conquered by Scythian barbarians, yet Shakespeare would be an immortal England, and would conquer countries, when the bones of her last sailor had kept their ghastly watch for ages in unhallowed ooze beside the quenched thunders of her navy.

Old Purchas in his "Pilgrims" tells of a sacred caste in India who, when they go out into the street, cry out, "Poo! Poo!" to warn all the world out of their way lest they should be defiled by something unclean. And it is just so that the understanding in its pride of success thinks to pooh-pooh all that it considers impractical and visionary. But whatever of life there is in man, except what comes of beef and pudding, is in the visionary and unpractical, and if it be not encouraged to find its activity or its solace in the production or enjoyment of art and beauty, if it be bewildered or thwarted by an outward profession of faith covering up a practical unbelief in anything higher and holier than the world of sense, it will find vent in such wretched holes and corners as table-tippings and mediums who sell news from heaven at a quarter of a dollar the item. Imagination cannot be banished out of the world. She may be made a kitchen-drudge, a Cinderella, but there are powers that watch over her. When her two proud sisters, the intellect and understanding, think her crouching over her ashes, she startles and charms by her splendid apparition, and Prince Soul will put up with no other bride.

The practical is a very good thing in its way — if it only be not another name for the worldly. To be absorbed in it is to eat of that insane root which the soldiers of Antonius found in their retreat from Parthia — which whoso tasted kept gathering sticks and stones as if they were some great matter till he died.

One is forced to listen, now and then, to a kind of talk which makes him feel as if this were the after-dinner time of the world, and mankind were doomed hereafter forever to that kind of contented materialism which comes to good stomachs with the nuts and raisins. The dozy old world has nothing to do now but stretch its legs under the mahogany, talk about stocks, and get rid of the hours as well as it can till bedtime. The centuries before us have drained the goblet of wisdom and beauty, and all we have left is to cast horoscopes in the dregs. But divine beauty, and the love of it, will never be without apostles and messengers on earth, till Time flings his hour-glass into the abyss as having no need to turn it longer to number the indistinguishable ages of Annihilation. It was a favorite speculation with the learned men of the sixteenth century that they had come upon the old age and decrepit second childhood of creation, and while they maundered, the soul of Shakespeare was just coming out of the eternal freshness of Deity, "trailing" such "clouds of glory" as would beggar a Platonic year of sunsets.

No; morning and the dewy prime are born into the earth again with every child. It is our fault if drought and dust usurp the noon. Every age says to her poets, like the mistress to her lover, "Tell me what I am like"; and, in proportion as it brings forth anything worth seeing, has need of seers and will have them. Our time is not an unpoetical one. We are in our heroic age, still face to face with the shaggy forces of unsubdued Nature, and we have our Theseuses and Perseuses, though they may be named Israel Putnam and Daniel Boone. It is nothing against us that we are a commercial people. Athens was a trading community; Dante and Titian were the growth of great marts, and England was already commercial when she produced Shakespeare.

This lesson I learn from the past: that grace and goodness, the fair, the noble, and the true, will never cease out of the world till the God from whom they emanate ceases out of it; that they manifest themselves in an eternal continuity of change to every generation of men, as new duties and occasions arise; that the sacred duty and noble office of the poet is to reveal and justify them to men; that so long as the soul endures, endures also the theme of new and unexampled song; that while there is grace in grace, love in love, and beauty in beauty, God will still send poets to find them and bear witness of them, and to hang their ideal portraitures in the gallery of memory. God with us is forever the mystical name of the hour that is passing. The lives of the great poets teach us that they were the men of their generation who felt most deeply the meaning of the present.

HUMOR, WIT, FUN, AND SATIRE

PREFATORY NOTE

In the winter of 1855, when Lowell was thirty-six years old, he gave a course of twelve lectures before the Lowell Institute in Boston. His subject was the English Poets, and the special topics of the successive lectures were: 1, "Poetry, and the Poetic Sentiment," illustrating the imaginative faculty; 2, "Piers Ploughman's Vision," as the first characteristically English poem; 3, "The Metrical Romances," marking the advent into our poetry of the sense of Beauty; 4, "The Ballads," especially as models of narrative diction; 5, Chaucer, as the poet of real life — the poet outside of nature; 6, Spenser, as the representative of the purely poetical; 7, Milton, as representing the imaginative; 8, Butler, as the wit; 9, Pope, as the poet of artificial life; 10, "On Poetic Diction"; 11, Wordsworth, as representing the egotistic imaginative, or the poet feeling himself in nature; 12, "On the Function and Prospects of Poetry."

These lectures were written rapidly, many of them during the period of delivery of the course; they bore marks of hastiness of composition, but they came from a full and rich mind, and they were the issues of familiar studies and long reflection. No such criticism, at once abundant in knowledge and in sympathetic insight, and distinguished by breadth of view, as well as by fluency, grace, and power of style, had been heard in America. They were listened to by large and enthusiastic audiences, and they did much to establish Lowell's position as the ablest of living critics of poetry, and, in many respects, as the foremost of American men of letters.

In the same year he was made Professor of Belles-Lettres in Harvard University, and after spending somewhat more

[33]

than a year in Europe, in special preparation, he entered in the autumn of 1856 upon the duties of the chair, which he continued to occupy till 1877, when he was appointed Minister of the United States to Spain.

During the years of his professorship he delivered numerous courses of lectures to his classes. Few of them were written out, but they were given more or less extemporaneously from full notes. The subject of these courses was in general the "Study of Literature," treating in different years of different special topics, from the literature of Northern to that of Southern Europe, from the Kalevala and the Niebelungen Lied to the Provençal poets; from Wolfram von Eschenbach to Rousseau; from the cycle of romances of Charlemagne and his peers to Dante and Shakespeare. Some of these lectures, or parts of them, were afterward prepared for publication, with such changes as were required to give them proper literary form; and the readers of Lowell's prose works know what gifts of native power, what large and solid acquisitions of learning, what wide and delightful survey of the field of life and of letters, are to be found in his essays on Shakespeare, on Dante, on Dryden, and on many another poet or prose writer. The abundance of his resources as critic in the highest sense have never been surpassed, at least in English literature.

But considerable portions of the earlier as well as of the later lectures remain unprinted, partly, no doubt, because his points of view changed with the growth of his learning, and the increasing depth as well as breadth of his vision. There is but little in manuscript which he would himself, I believe, have been inclined to print without substantial change. Yet these unprinted remains contain so much that seems to me to possess permanent value that, after some question and hesitation, I have come to the conclusion that selections from them should be published. The fragments must be read with the fact constantly held in mind that they do not always represent Lowell's mature opinions;

that, in some instances, they give but the first form of thoughts developed in other connections in one or other of his later essays; that they have not received his last revision; that they have the form of discourse addressed to the ear, rather than that of literary work finished for the eye.

If so read, I trust that the reader, while he may find little in them to increase Lowell's well-established reputation, may find much in them to confirm a high estimate of his position as one of the rare masters of English prose as well as one of the most capable of critics; much to interest him alike in their intrinsic character, and in their illustration of the life and thought of the writer; and much to make him feel a keen regret that they are the final contributions of their author to the treasures of English literature.

Charles Eliot Norton

HIPPEL, the German satirist, divides the life of man into five periods, according to the ruling desires which successively displace each other in the human soul. Our first longing, he says, is for trousers, the second for a watch, the third for an angel in pink muslin, the fourth for money, and the fifth for a "place" in the country. I think he has overlooked one, which I should be inclined to place second in point of time — the ambition to escape the gregarious nursery, and to be master of a chamber to one's self.

How charming is the memory of that cloistered freedom, of that independence, wide as desire, though, perhaps, only ten feet by twelve! How much of future tastes and powers lay in embryo there in that small chamber! It is the egg of the coming life. There the young sailor pores over the "Narratives of Remarkable Shipwrecks," his longing heightened as the storm roars on the roof, or blows its trumpet in the chimney. There the unfledged naturalist gathers his menagerie, and empties his pockets of bugs and turtles that awaken the ignorant animosity of the housemaid. There the commencing chemist rehearses the experiment of Schwarz, and singes off those eyebrows which shall some day feel the cool shadow of the discoverer's laurel. There the antiquary begins his collections with a bullet from Bunker Hill, as genuine as the epistles of Phalaris, or a button from the coat-tail of Columbus, late the property of a neighboring scarecrow, and sold to him by a schoolmate, who thus lays the foundation of that colossal fortune which is to make his children the ornaments of society. There the potential Dibdin or Dowse gathers his library on a single pendulous shelf — more fair to him than the hanging gardens of Babylon. There stand "Robinson Crusoe," and "Gulliver," perhaps "Gil Blas," Goldsmith's Histories of Greece and Rome, "Original Poems for Infant Minds," the "Parent's Assistant," and (for Sundays) the "Shepherd of Salisbury Plain," with other narratives of the excellent Mrs. Hannah More too much neglected in maturer life. With these are admitted also "Viri Romæ," Nepos, Florus, Phædrus, and even the Latin grammar, because they *count*, playing here upon these mimic boards the silent but awful part of second and third conspirators, a rôle in after years assumed by statelier and more celebrated volumes — the "books without which no gentleman's library can be complete."

I remember (for I must call my memory back from this garrulous rookery of the past to some perch nearer the matter in hand) that when I was first installed lord of such a manor, and found myself the Crusoe of that remote attic-island, which for near thirty years was to be my unmolested hermitage, I cast about for works of art with which to adorn it. The garret, that El Dorado of boys, supplied me with some prints which had once been the chief ornament of my great-grandfather's study, but which the growth of taste or luxury had banished from story to story till they had arrived where malice could pursue them no farther. These were heads of ancient worthies [1] — Plato, Pythagoras, Socrates, Seneca, and Cicero, whom, from a prejudice acquired at school, I shortly banished again with a *quousque tandem!* Besides those I have mentioned, there were Democritus and Heraclitus, which last, in those days less the slave of tradition, I called Heraclïtus — an error which my excellent schoolmaster (I thank him for it) would have expelled from my head by the judicious application of a counter-irritant; for he

---

[1] Some readers may recall the reference to these "heads of ancient wise men" in "An Interview with Miles Standish." — C. E. N.

regarded the birth as a kind of usher to the laurel, as indeed the true tree of knowledge, whose advantages could Adam have enjoyed during early life, he had known better than to have yielded to the temptation of any other.

Well, over my chimney hung those two antithetical philosophers — the one showing his teeth in an eternal laugh, while the tears on the cheek of the other forever ran, and yet, like the leaves on Keats's Grecian urn, could never be shed. I used to wonder at them sometimes, believing, as I did firmly, that to weep and laugh had been respectively the sole business of their lives. I was puzzled to think which had the harder time of it, and whether it were more painful to be under contract for the delivery of so many tears *per diem*, or to compel that ἀνήριθμον γέλασμα.[1] I confess, I pitied them both; for if it be difficult to produce on demand what Laura Matilda would call the "tender dew of sympathy," he is also deserving of compassion who is expected to be funny whether he will or no. As I grew older, and learned to look on the two heads as types, they gave rise to many reflections, raising a question perhaps impossible to solve: whether the vices and follies of men were to be washed away, or exploded by a broadside of honest laughter. I believe it is Southwell who says that Mary Magdalene went to Heaven by water,

[1] Countless — *i.e.*, perpetual — smile.

and it is certain that the tears that people shed
for themselves are apt to be sincere; but I doubt
whether we are to be saved by any amount of vicarious salt water, and, though the philosophers
should weep us into another Noah's flood, yet commonly men have lumber enough of self-conceit to
build a raft of, and can subsist a good while on
that beautiful charity for their own weaknesses in
which the nerves of conscience are embedded and
cushioned, as in similar physical straits they can
upon their fat.

On the other hand, man has a wholesome dread of
laughter, as he is the only animal capable of that
phenomenon — for the laugh of the hyena is pronounced by those who have heard it to be no joke,
and to be classed with those γέλασματα ἀγέλαστα
which are said to come from the other side of the
mouth. Whether, as Shaftesbury will have it, ridicule
be absolutely the test of truth or no, we may admit
it to be relatively so, inasmuch as by the *reductio ad
absurdum* it often shows that abstract truth may
become falsehood, if applied to the practical affairs
of life, because its relation to other truths equally
important, or to human nature, has been overlooked.
For men approach truth from the circumference,
and, acquiring a knowledge at most of one or two
points of that circle of which God is the centre, are
apt to assume that the fixed point from which it

is described is that where they stand. Moreover,
"Ridentem dicere verum, quid vetat?"

I side rather with your merry fellow than with
Dr. Young when he says:

> Laughter, though never censured yet as sin,
>
> . . . .
>
> Is half immoral, be it much indulged;
> By venting spleen, or dissipating thought,
> It shows a scorner, or it makes a fool;
> And sins, as hurting others or ourselves.
>
> . . . .
>
> Yet would'st thou laugh (but at thine own expense),
> This counsel strange should I presume to give —
> "Retire, and read thy Bible, to be gay."

With shame I confess it, Dr. Young's "Night
Thoughts" have given me as many hearty laughs
as any humorous book I ever read.

Men of one idea, — that is, who have one idea at
a time, — men who accomplish great results, men
of action, reformers, saints, martyrs, are inevitably
destitute of humor; and if the idea that inspires them
be great and noble, they are impervious to it. But
through the perversity of human affairs it not in-
frequently happens that men are possessed by a
single idea, and that a small and rickety one — some
seven months' child of thought — that maintains a
querulous struggle for life, sometimes to the dis-
quieting of a whole neighborhood. These last commonly need no satirist, but, to use a common phrase,
make themselves absurd, as if Nature intended them

for parodies on some of her graver productions. For example, how could the attempt to make application of mystical prophecy to current events be rendered more ridiculous than when we read that two hundred years ago it was a leading point in the teaching of Lodowick Muggleton, a noted heresiarch, "that one John Robins was the last great antichrist and son of perdition spoken of by the Apostle in Thessalonians"? I remember also an eloquent and distinguished person who, beginning with the axiom that all the disorders of this microcosm, the body, had their origin in diseases of the soul, carried his doctrine to the extent of affirming that all derangements of the macrocosm likewise were due to the same cause. Hearing him discourse, you would have been well-nigh persuaded that you had a kind of complicity in the spots upon the sun, had he not one day condensed his doctrine into an epigram which made it instantly ludicrous. "I consider myself," exclaimed he, "personally responsible for the obliquity of the earth's axis." A prominent Comeouter once told me, with a look of indescribable satisfaction, that he had just been kicked out of a Quaker meeting. "I have had," he said, "Calvinistic kicks and Unitarian kicks, Congregational, Presbyterian, and Episcopalian kicks, but I never succeeded in getting a Quaker kick before." Could the fanaticism of the collectors of worthless rarities be more admirably caricatured than thus unconsciously by our passive enthusiast?

I think no one can go through a museum of natural curiosities, or see certain animals, without a feeling that Nature herself has a sense of the comic. There are some donkeys that one can scarce look at without laughing (perhaps on Cicero's principle of the *haruspex haruspicem*) and feeling inclined to say, "My good fellow, if you will keep my secret I will keep yours." In human nature, the sense of the comic seems to be implanted to keep man sane, and preserve a healthy balance between body and soul. But for this, the sorcerer Imagination or the witch Enthusiasm would lead us an endless dance.

The advantage of the humorist is that he cannot be a man of one idea — for the essence of humor lies in the contrast of two. He is the universal disenchanter. He makes himself quite as much the subject of ironical study as his neighbor. Is he inclined to fancy himself a great poet, or an original thinker, he remembers the man who dared not sit down because a certain part of him was made of glass, and muses smilingly, "There are many forms of hypochondria." This duality in his mind which constitutes his intellectual advantage is the defect of his character. He is futile in action because in every path he is confronted by the horns of an eternal dilemma, and is apt to come to the conclusion that nothing is very

[42]

much worth the while. If he be independent of exertion, his life commonly runs to waste. If he turn author, it is commonly from necessity; Fielding wrote for money, and "Don Quixote" was the fruit of a debtors' prison.

It seems to be an instinct of human nature to analyze, to define, and to classify. We like to have things conveniently labelled and laid away in the mind, and feel as if we knew them better when we have named them. And so to a certain extent we do. The mere naming of things by their appearance is science; the knowing them by their qualities is wisdom; and the being able to express them by some intense phrase which combines appearance and quality as they affect the imagination through the senses by impression, is poetry. A great part of criticism is scientific, but as the laws of art are only echoes of the laws of nature, it is possible in this direction also to arrive at real knowledge, or, if not so far as that, at some kind of classification that may help us toward that excellent property — compactness of mind.

Addison has given the pedigree of humor: the union of truth and goodness produces wit; that of wit with wrath produces humor. We should say that this was rather a pedigree of satire. For what trace of wrath is there in the humor of Chaucer, Shakespeare, Rabelais, Cervantes, Sterne, Fielding, or

Thackeray? The absence of wrath is the characteristic of all of them. Ben Jonson says that

> When some one peculiar quality
> Doth so possess a man that it doth draw
> All his affects, his spirits, and his powers
> In their constructions all to run one way,
> This may be truly said to be a humor.

But this, again, is the definition of a humorous character, — of a good subject for the humorist, — such
as Don Quixote, for example.

Humor — taken in the sense of the faculty to
perceive what is humorous, and to give it expression
— seems to be greatly a matter of temperament.
Hence, probably, its name. It is something quite indefinable, diffused through the whole nature of the
man; so that it is related of the great comic actors
that the audience begin to laugh as soon as they
show their faces, or before they have spoken a word.

The sense of the humorous is certainly closely
allied with the understanding, and no race has shown
so much of it on the whole as the English, and next
to them the Spanish — both inclined to gravity. Let
us not be ashamed to confess that, if we find the
tragedy a bore, we take the profoundest satisfaction
in the farce. It is a mark of sanity. Humor, in its
highest level, is the sense of comic contradiction
which arises from the perpetual comment which the
understanding makes upon the impressions received

through the imagination. Richter, himself, a great humorist, defines it thus:

Humor is the sublime reversed; it brings down the great in order to set the little beside it, and elevates the little in order to set it beside the great — that it may annihilate both, because in the presence of the infinite all are alike nothing. Only the universal, only totality, moves its deepest spring, and from this universality, the leading component of Humor, arise the mildness and forbearance of the humorist toward the individual, who is lost in the mass of little consequence; this also distinguishes the Humorist from the Scoffer.

We find it very natural accordingly to speak of the breadth of humor, while wit is, by the necessity of its being, as narrow as a flash of lightning, and as sudden. Humor may pervade a whole page without our being able to put our finger on any passage, and say, "It is here." Wit must sparkle and snap in every line, or it is nothing. When the wise deacon shook his head, and said that "there was a good deal of human natur' in man," he might have added that there was a good deal more in some men than in others. Those who have the largest share of it may be humorists, but wit demands only a clear and nimble intellect, presence of mind, and a happy faculty of expression. This perfection of phrase, this neatness, is an essential of wit, because its effect must be instantaneous; whereas humor is often diffuse and roundabout, and its impression cumulative, like the poison of arsenic. As Galiani said of Nature that her dice were always loaded, so the wit must throw sixes every time. And what the same Galiani gave as a definition of sublime oratory may be applied to its dexterity of phrase: "It is the art of saying everything without being clapt in the Bastile, in a country where it is forbidden to say anything." Wit must also have the quality of unexpectedness. "Sometimes," says Barrow, "an affected simplicity, sometimes a presumptuous bluntness, gives it being. Sometimes it rises only from a lucky hitting upon what is strange, sometimes from a crafty wresting of obvious matter to the purpose. Often it consisteth in one knows not what, and springeth up one can hardly tell how. Its ways are unaccountable and inexplicable, being answerable to the numberless rovings of fancy and windings of language."

That wit does not consist in the discovery of a merely unexpected likeness or even contrast in word or thought, is plain if we look at what is called a *conceit*, which has all the qualities of wit — except wit. For example, Warner, a contemporary of Shakespeare, wrote a long poem called "Albion's England," which had an immense contemporary popularity, and is not without a certain value still to the student of language. In this I find a perfect specimen of what is called a conceit. Queen Eleanor strikes Fair Rosamond, and Warner says,

> Hard was the heart that gave the blow,
> Soft were those lips that bled.[1]

This is bad as fancy for precisely the same reason that it would be good as a pun. The comparison is unintentionally wanting in logic, just as a pun is intentionally so. To make the contrast what it should have been, — to make it coherent, if I may use that term of a contrast, — it should read:

> Hard was the *hand* that gave the blow,
> Soft were those lips that bled,

for otherwise there is no identity of meaning in the word "hard" as applied to the two nouns it qualifies, and accordingly the proper logical copula is wanting. Of the same kind is the conceit which belongs, I believe, to our countryman General Morris:

> Her heart and morning broke together
> In tears,

which is so preposterous that had it been intended for fun we might almost have laughed at it. Here again the logic is unintentionally violated in the word *broke*, and the sentence becomes absurd, though not funny. Had it been applied to a merchant ruined by the failure of the United States Bank, we should at once see the ludicrousness of it, though here, again, there would be no true wit:

[1] This, and one or two of the following illustrations, were used again by Mr. Lowell in his "Shakespeare Once More": *Works* (Riverside edition), III, 53.

His heart and Biddle broke together
On 'change.

Now let me give an instance of true fancy from Butler, the author of "Hudibras," certainly the greatest wit who ever wrote English, and whose wit is so profound, so purely the wit of thought, that we might almost rank him with the humorists, but that his genius was cramped with a contemporary, and therefore transitory, subject. Butler says of loyalty that it is

True as the dial to the sun
Although it be not shined upon.

Now what is the difference between this and the examples from Warner and Morris which I have just quoted? Simply that the comparison turning upon the word *true*, the mind is satisfied, because the analogy between the word as used morally and as used physically is so perfect as to leave no gap for the reasoning faculty to jolt over. But it is precisely this jolt, not so violent as to be displeasing, violent enough to discompose our thoughts with an agreeable sense of surprise, which it is the object of a pun to give us. Wit of this kind treats logic with every possible outward demonstration of respect — "keeps the word of promise to the ear, and breaks it to the sense." Dean Swift's famous question to the man carrying the hare, "Pray, sir, is that your own hare or a wig?" is perfect in its way. Here there is an

absolute identity of sound with an equally absolute
and therefore ludicrous disparity of meaning. Hood
abounds in examples of this sort of fun — only that
his analogies are of a more subtle and perplexing
kind. In his elegy on the old sailor he says,

> His head was turned, and so he chewed
> His pigtail till he died.

This is inimitable, like all the best of Hood's puns.
To the ear it is perfect, but so soon as you attempt to
realize it to yourself, the mind is involved in an in-
extricable confusion of comical *non sequiturs*. And
yet observe the gravity with which the forms of
reason are kept up in the "and so." Like this is the
peddler's recommendation of his ear-trumpet:

> I don't pretend with horns of mine,
> Like some in the advertising line,
> To magnify sounds on such marvellous scales
> That the sounds of a cod seem as large as a whale's.
>
> There was Mrs. F. so very deaf
> That she might have worn a percussion cap
> And been knocked on the head without hearing it snap.
> Well, I sold her a horn, and the very next day
> She heard from her husband in Botany Bay.

Again, his definition of deafness:

> Deaf as the dog's ears in Enfield's "Speaker."

So, in his description of the hardships of the wild
beasts in the menagerie,

> Who could not even prey
> In their own way,

and the monkey-reformer who resolved to set them all free, beginning with the lion; but

> Pug had only half unbolted Nero,
> When Nero bolted him.

In Hood there is almost always a combination of wit and fun, the wit always suggesting the remote association of ideas, and the fun jostling together the most obvious concords of sound and discords of sense. Hood's use of words reminds one of the kaleidoscope. Throw them down in a heap, and they are the most confused jumble of unrelated bits; but once in the magical tube of his fancy, and, with a shake and a turn, they assume figures that have the absolute perfection of geometry. In the droll complaint of the lover,

> Perhaps it was right to dissemble your love,
> But why did you kick me down-stairs?

the self-sparing charity of phrase that could stretch the meaning of the word "dissemble" so as to make it cover so violent a process as kicking downstairs has the true zest, the tang, of contradiction and surprise. Hood, not content with such a play upon ideas, would bewitch the whole sentence with plays upon words also. His fancy has the enchantment of Huon's horn, and sets the gravest conceptions a-capering in a way that makes us laugh in spite of ourselves.

Andrew Marvell's satire upon the Dutch is a capital instance of wit as distinguished from fun. It

rather exercises than tickles the mind, so full is it of
quaint fancy:

> Holland, that scarce deserves the name of land,
> As but the offscouring of the British sand,
> And so much earth as was contributed
> By English pilots when they heaved the lead,
> Or what by ocean's slow alluvium fell
> Of shipwrecked cockle and the muscle-shell;
> This indigestful vomit of the sea
> Fell to the Dutch by just propriety.
>
> Glad, then, as miners who have found the ore
> They, with mad labor, fished their land to shore,
> And dived as desperately for each piece
> Of earth as if 't had been of ambergreese
> Collecting anxiously small loads of clay,
> Less than what building swallows bear away,
> Or than those pills which sordid beetles roll,
> Transfusing into them their sordid soul.
>
> How did they rivet with gigantic piles
> Thorough the centre their new-catchèd miles,
> And to the stake a struggling country bound,
> Where barking waves still bait the forcèd ground!
>
> Yet still his claim the injured ocean laid,
> And oft at leap-frog o'er their steeples played,
> As if on purpose it on land had come
> To show them what's their *mare liberum;*
> The fish ofttimes the burgher dispossessed,
> And sate, not as a meat, but as a guest;
> And oft the Tritons and the sea-nymphs tan
> Whole shoals of Dutch served up as Caliban,
> And, as they over the new level ranged,
> For pickled herring pickled Heeren changed.
> Therefore necessity, that first made kings,
> Something like government among them brings;

> And as among the blind the blinkard reigns
> So rules among the drownèd he that drains;
> Who best could know to pump on earth a leak,
> Him they their lord and Country's Father speak.
> To make a bank was a great plot of state,
> Invent a shovel and be a magistrate;
> Hence some small dykegrave, unperceived, invades
> The power, and grows, as 't were, a king of spades.

I have cited this long passage not only because Marvell (both in his serious and comic verse) is a great favorite of mine, but because it is as good an illustration as I know how to find of that fancy flying off into extravagance, and that nice compactness of expression, that constitute genuine wit. On the other hand, Smollett is only funny, hardly witty, where he condenses all his wrath against the Dutch into an epigram of two lines:

> Amphibious creatures, sudden be your fall,
> May man undam you and God damn you all.

Of satirists I have hitherto said nothing, because some, perhaps the most eminent of them, do not come under the head either of wit or humor. With them, as Juvenal said of himself, "facit indignatio versus," and wrath is the element, as a general rule, neither of wit nor humor. Swift, in the epitaph he wrote for himself, speaks of the grave as a place "ubi saeva indignatio cor ulterius lacerare nequeat," and this hints at the sadness which makes the ground of all humor. There is certainly humor in "Gulliver," especially in the chapters about the Yahoos, where the

horses are represented as the superior beings, and
disgusted at the filthiness of the creatures in human
shape. But commonly Swift, too, must be ranked
with the wits, if we measure him rather by what
he wrote than by what he was. Take this for an
example from the "Day of Judgment":

> With a whirl of thought oppressed
> I sank from reverie to rest,
> A horrid vision seized my head,
> I saw the graves give up their dead!
> Jove, armed with terrors, burst the skies,
> And thunder roars, and lightning flies!
> Amazed, confused, its fate unknown,
> The world stands trembling at his throne!
> While each pale sinner hung his head,
> Jove, nodding, shook the heavens, and said:
> "Offending race of human kind;
> By nature, reason, learning, blind,
> You who through frailty stepped aside,
> And you who never fell through pride,
> You who in different sects were shammed,
> And come to see each other damned
> (So some folks told you — but they knew
> No more of Jove's designs than you) —
> The world's mad business now is o'er,
> And I resent these pranks no more —
> *I* to such blockheads set my wit!
> *I* damn such fools! Go, go! you're bit!"

The unexpectedness of the conclusion here, after
the somewhat solemn preface, is entirely of the
essence of wit. So, too, is the sudden flirt of the
scorpion's tail to sting you. It is almost the opposite
of humor in one respect — namely, that it would

make us think the solemnest things in life were sham, whereas it is the sham-solemn ones which humor delights in exposing. This further difference is also true: that wit makes you laugh once, and loses some of its comicality (though none of its point) with every new reading, while humor grows droller and droller the oftener we read it. If we cannot safely deny that Swift was a humorist, we may at least say that he was one in whom humor had gone through the stage of acetous fermentation and become rancid. We should never forget that he died mad. Satirists of this kind, while they have this quality of true humor, that they contrast a higher with a lower, differ from their nobler brethren inasmuch as their comparison is always to the disadvantage of the higher. They purposely disenchant us — while the others rather show us how sad a thing it is to be disenchanted at all.

Ben Jonson, who had in respect of sturdy good sense very much the same sort of mind as his namesake Samuel, and whose "Discoveries," as he calls them, are well worth reading for the sound criticism they contain, says:

The parts of a comedy are the same with [those of] a tragedy, and the end is partly the same; for they both delight and teach: the comics are called *didaskaloi* [1] of the Greeks, no less than the tragics. Nor is the moving of

---

[1] Teachers.

laughter always the end of comedy; that is rather a fowling for the people's delight, or their fooling. For, as Aristotle says rightly, the moving of laughter is a fault in comedy, a kind of turpitude that depraves some part of a man's nature without a disease. As a wry face moves laughter, or a deformed vizard, or a rude clown dressed in a lady's habit and using her actions; we dislike and scorn such representations, which made the ancient philosophers ever think laughter unfitting in a wise man. So that what either in the words or sense of an author, or in the language and actions of men, is awry or depraved, does strongly stir mean affections, and provoke for the most part to laughter. And therefore it was clear that all insolent and obscene speeches, jests upon the best men, injuries to particular persons, perverse and sinister sayings (and the rather, unexpected) in the old comedy did move laughter, especially where it did imitate any dishonesty, and scurrility came forth in the place of wit; which, who understands the nature and genius of laughter cannot but perfectly know.

He then goes on to say of Aristophanes that

he expressed all the moods and figures of what was ridiculous, oddly. In short, as vinegar is not accounted good till the wine be corrupted, so jests that are true and natural seldom raise laughter with that beast the multitude. They love nothing that is right and proper. The farther it runs from reason or possibility, with them the better it is.

In the latter part of this it is evident that Ben is speaking with a little bitterness. His own comedies are too rigidly constructed according to Aristotle's dictum, that the moving of laughter was a fault in comedy. I like the passage as an illustration of a fact undeniably true, that Shakespeare's humor was altogether a new thing upon the stage, and also as showing that satirists (for such were also the writers of comedy) were looked upon rather as censors and moralists than as movers of laughter. Dante, accordingly, himself in this sense the greatest of satirists, in putting Horace among the five great poets in limbo, qualifies him with the title of *satiro*.

But if we exclude the satirists, what are we to do with Aristophanes? Was he not a satirist, and in some sort also a censor? Yes; but, as it appears to me, of a different kind, as well as in a different degree, from any other ancient. I think it is plain that he wrote his comedies not only to produce certain political, moral, and even literary ends, but for the fun of the thing. I am so poor a Grecian that I have no doubt I miss three quarters of what is most characteristic of him. But even through the fog of the Latin on the opposite page I can make out more or less of the true lineaments of the man. I can see that he was a master of language, for it becomes alive under his hands — puts forth buds and blossoms like the staff of Joseph, as it does always when it feels the hand and recognizes the touch of its legitimate sovereigns. Those prodigious combinations of his are like some of the strange polyps we hear of that seem a single organism; but cut them into as many parts as you please, each has a life of its own and stirs with independent being. There is nothing that words will not do for him; no service seems too mean or too high. And then his abundance! He puts one in mind of the definition of a competence by the only man I ever saw who had the true flavor of Falstaff in him — "a million a minute and your expenses paid." As Burns said of himself, "The rhymes come skelpin, rank and file." Now they are as graceful and sinuous as water-nymphs, and now they come tumbling head over heels, throwing somersaults, like clowns in the circus, with a "Here we are!" I can think of nothing like it but Rabelais, who had the same extraordinary gift of getting all the *go* out of words. They do not merely play with words; they romp with them, tickle them, tease them, and somehow the words seem to like it.

I dare say there may be as much fancy and fun in "The Clouds" or "The Birds," but neither of them seems so rich to me as "The Frogs," nor does the fun anywhere else climb so high or dwell so long in the region of humor as here. Lucian makes Greek mythology comic, to be sure, but he has nothing like the scene in "The Frogs," where Bacchus is terrified with the strange outcries of a procession celebrating his own mysteries, and of whose dithyrambic songs it is plain he can make neither head nor tail. Here is humor of the truest metal, and, so far as we can guess, the first example of it. Here is the true humorous contrast between the ideal god and the god with human weaknesses and follies as he had been degraded in the popular conception. And is it too absurd to be within the limits even of comic probability? Is it even so absurd as those hand-mills for grinding out so many prayers a minute which Huc and Gabet saw in Tartary?

Cervantes was born on October 9, 1547, and died on April 23, 1616, on the same day as Shakespeare. He is, I think, beyond all question, the greatest of humorists. Whether he intended it or not, — and I am inclined to believe he did, — he has typified in Don Quixote, and Sancho Panza his esquire, the two component parts of the human mind and shapers of human character — the imagination and understanding. There is a great deal more than this; for what is positive and intentional in a truly great book is often little in comparison with what is accidental and suggested. The plot is of the meagrest. A country gentleman of La Mancha, living very much by himself, and continually feeding his fancy with the romances of chivalry, becomes at last the victim of a monomania on this one subject, and resolves to revive the order of chivalry in his own proper person. He persuades a somewhat prosaic neighbor of his to accompany him as squire. They sally forth, and meet with various adventures, from which they reap no benefit but the sad experience of plentiful rib-roasting. Now if this were all of "Don Quixote," it would

be simply broad farce, as it becomes in Butler's
parody of it in Sir Hudibras and Ralpho so far as
mere external characteristics are concerned. The
latter knight and his squire are the most glaring
absurdities, without any sufficient reason for their
being at all, or for their adventures, except that they
furnished Butler with mouthpieces for his own wit
and wisdom. They represent nothing, and are intended to represent nothing.

I confess that, in my judgment, Don Quixote is
the most perfect character ever drawn. As Sir John
Falstaff is, in a certain sense, always a gentleman, —
that is, as he is guilty of no crime that is technically
held to operate in defeasance of his title to that
name as a man of the world, — so is Don Quixote, in
everything that does not concern his monomania, a
perfect gentleman and a good Christian besides. He
is not the merely technical gentleman of three de-
scents — but the *true* gentleman, such a gentleman
as only purity, disinterestedness, generosity, and fear
of God can make. And with what consummate skill
are the boundaries of his mania drawn! He only be-
lieves in enchantment just so far as is necessary to
account to Sancho and himself for the ill event of all
his exploits. He always reasons rightly, as madmen
do, from his own premises. And this is the reason I
object to Cervantes's treatment of him in the second
part — which followed the other after an interval of

nearly eight years. For, except in so far as they delude themselves, monomaniacs are as sane as other people, and besides shocking our feelings, the tricks played on the Don at the Duke's castle are so transparent that he could never have been taken in by them.

Don Quixote is the everlasting type of the disappointment which sooner or later always overtakes the man who attempts to accomplish ideal good by material means. Sancho, on the other hand, with his proverbs, is the type of the man with common sense. He always sees things in the daylight of reason. He is never taken in by his master's theory of enchanters, — although superstitious enough to believe such things possible, — but he *does* believe, despite all reverses, in his promises of material prosperity and advancement. The island that has been promised him always floats before him like the air-drawn dagger before Macbeth, and beckons him on. The whole character is exquisite. And, fitly enough, when he at last becomes governor of his imaginary island of Barataria, he makes an excellent magistrate — because statesmanship depends for its success so much less on abstract principle than on precisely that traditional wisdom in which Sancho was rich.

THE FIVE INDISPENSABLE AUTHORS
(HOMER, DANTE, CERVANTES, GOETHE
SHAKESPEARE)

THE study of literature, that it may be fruitful, that it may not result in a mere gathering of names and dates and phrases, must be a study of ideas and not of words, of periods rather than of men, or only of such men as are great enough or individual enough to reflect as much light upon their age as they in turn receive from it. To know literature as the elder Disraeli knew it is at best only an amusement, an accomplishment, great, indeed, for the dilettante, but valueless for the scholar. Detached facts are nothing in themselves, and become of worth only in their relation to one another. It is little, for example, to know the date of Shakespeare: something more that he and Cervantes were contemporaries; and a great deal that he grew up in a time fermenting with reformation in Church and State, when the intellectual impulse from the invention of printing had scarcely reached its climax, and while the New World stung the imaginations of men with its immeasurable promise and its temptations to daring adventure. Facts in themselves are clumsy and cumbrous — the cowry-currency of isolated and uninventive men; generalizations, conveying great sums of knowledge in a little

[61]

space, mark the epoch of free interchange of ideas, of higher culture, and of something better than provincial scholarship.

But generalizations, again, though in themselves the work of a happier moment, of some genetic flash in the brain of man, gone before one can say it lightens, are the result of ideas slowly gathered and long steeped and clarified in the mind, each in itself a composite of the carefully observed relations of separate and seemingly disparate facts. What is the pedigree of almost all great fortunes? Through vast combinations of trade, forlorn hopes of speculation, you trace them up to a clear head and a self-earned sixpence. It is the same with all large mental accumulations: they begin with a steady brain and the first solid result of thought, however small — the nucleus of speculation. The true aim of the scholar is not to crowd his memory, but to classify and sort it, till what was a heap of chaotic curiosities becomes a museum of science.

It may well be questioned whether the invention of printing, while it democratized information, has not also levelled the ancient aristocracy of thought. By putting a library within the power of every one, it has taught men to depend on their shelves rather than on their brains; it has supplanted a strenuous habit of thinking with a loose indolence of reading which relaxes the muscular fiber of the mind. When men had few books, they mastered those few; but now the multitude of books lord it over the man. The costliness of books was a great refiner of literature. Men disposed of single volumes by will with as many provisions and precautions as if they had been great landed estates. A mitre would hardly have overjoyed Petrarch as much as did the finding of a copy of Virgil. The problem for the scholar was formerly how to acquire books; for us it is how to get rid of them. Instead of gathering, we must sift. When Confucius made his collection of Chinese poems, he saved but three hundred and ten out of more than three thousand, and it has consequently survived until our day.

In certain respects the years do our weeding for us. In our youth we admire the verses which answer our mood; as we grow older we like those better which speak to our experience; at last we come to look only upon that as poetry which appeals to that original nature in us which is deeper than all moods and wiser than all experience. Before a man is forty he has broken many idols, and the milestones of his intellectual progress are the gravestones of dead and buried enthusiasms of his dethroned gods.

There are certain books which it is necessary to read; but they are very few. Looking at the matter from an æsthetic point of view, merely, I should say that thus far one man had been able to use types so universal, and to draw figures so cosmopolitan, that they are equally true in all languages and equally acceptable to the whole Indo-European branch, at least, of the human family. That man is Homer, and there needs, it seems to me, no further proof of his individual existence than this very fact of the solitary unapproachableness of the "Iliad" and the "Odyssey." The more wonderful they are, the more likely to be the work of one person. Nowhere is the purely natural man presented to us so nobly and sincerely as in these poems. Not far below these I should place the "Divina Commedia" of Dante, in which the history of the spiritual man is sketched with equal command of material and grandeur of outline. Don Quixote stands upon the same level, and receives the same universal appreciation. Here we have the spiritual and the natural man set before us in humorous contrast. In the knight and his squire Cervantes has typified the two opposing poles of our dual nature — the imagination and the understanding as they appear in contradiction. This is the only comprehensive satire ever written, for it is utterly independent of time, place, and manners. Faust gives us the natural history of the human intellect, Mephistopheles being merely the projected impersonation of that scepticism which is the invariable result of a purely intellectual culture. These four books are the only ones in which universal facts of human nature and experience are ideally represented. They can, therefore, never be displaced. Whatever moral significance there may be in certain episodes of the "Odyssey," the man of the Homeric poems is essentially the man of the senses and the understanding, to whom the other world is alien and therefore repulsive. There is nothing that demonstrates this more clearly, as there is nothing, in my judgment, more touching and picturesque in all poetry, than that passage in the eleventh book of the "Odyssey," where the shade of Achilles tells Ulysses that he would rather be the poorest shepherd-boy on a Grecian hill than king over the unsubstantial shades of Hades. Dante's poem, on the other hand, sets forth the passage of man from the world of sense to that of spirit; in other words, his moral conversion. It is Dante relating his experience in the great camp-meeting of mankind, but relating it, by virtue of his genius, so representatively that it is no longer the story of one man, but of all men. Then comes Cervantes, showing the perpetual and comic contradiction between the spiritual and the natural man in actual life, marking the transition from the age of the imagination to that of the intellect; and, lastly, Goethe, the poet of a period in which a purely intellectual culture reached its maximum of development, depicts its one-sidedness, and its consequent failure. These books, then, are not national, but human, and record certain phases of man's nature, certain stages of his moral progress. They are gospels in the lay bible of the race. It will remain for the future poet to write the epic of the complete man, as it remains for the future world to afford the example of his entire and harmonious development.

I have not mentioned Shakespeare, because his works come under a different category. Though they mark the very highest level of human genius, they yet represent no special epoch in the history of the individual mind. The man of Shakespeare is always the man of actual life as he is acted upon by the worlds of sense and of spirit under certain definite conditions. We all of us *may* be in the position of Macbeth or Othello or Hamlet, and we appreciate their sayings and deeds potentially, so to speak, rather than actually, through the sympathy of our common nature and not of our experience. But with the four books I have mentioned our relation is a very different one. We all of us grow up through the Homeric period of the senses; we all feel, at some time, sooner or later, the need of something higher, and, like Dante, shape our theory of the divine government of the universe; we all with Cervantes discover the rude contrast between the ideal and real, and with Goethe the unattainableness of the highest good through the intellect alone. Therefore I set these books by themselves. I do not mean that we read them, or for their full enjoyment need to read them, in this light; but I believe that this fact of their universal and perennial application to our consciousness and our experience accounts for their permanence, and insures their immortality.

THE IMAGINATION [1]

IMAGINATION is the wings of the mind; the understanding, its feet. With these it may climb high, but
can never soar into that ampler ether and diviner air
whence the eye dominates so uncontrolled a prospect
on every hand. Through imagination alone is something like a creative power possible to man. It is the
same in Æschylus as in Shakespeare, though the
form of its manifestation varies in some outward
respects from age to age. Being the faculty of vision,
it is the essential part of expression also, which is the
office of all art.

But in comparing ancient with modern imaginative literature, certain changes especially strike us,
and chief among them a stronger infusion of sentiment and what we call the picturesque. I shall endeavor to illustrate this by a few examples. But
first let us discuss imagination itself, and give some
instances of its working.

"Art," says Lord Verulam, "is man added to
Nature" (*homo additus naturæ*); and we may mod-
ernize his statement, and adapt it to the demands of
æsthetics, if we define art to be Nature infused with

[1] [A small portion of this lecture appeared at the time of its
delivery, in January, 1855, in a report printed in the *Boston Daily
Advertiser*.]

and shaped by the imaginative faculty of man; thus, as Bacon says elsewhere, "conforming the shows of things to the desires of the mind." Art always platonizes: it results from a certain finer instinct for form, order, proportion, a certain keener sense of the rhythm there is in the eternal flow of the world about us, and its products take shape around some idea preëxistent in the mind, are quickened into life by it, and strive always (cramped and hampered as they are by the limitations and conditions of human nature, of individual temperament, and outward circumstances) toward ideal perfection — toward what Michelangelo called

> Ideal form, the universal mould.

Shakespeare, whose careless generalizations have often the exactness of scientific definitions, tells us that

> The lunatic, the lover, and the poet,
> Are of imagination all compact;

that

> as imagination bodies forth
> The forms of things unknown, the poet's pen
> Turns them to shapes, and gives to airy nothing
> A local habitation and a name.

And a little before he had told us that

> Lovers and madmen have such seething brains,
> Such shaping fantasies, that apprehend
> More than cool reason ever comprehends.

Plato had said before him (in his "Ion") that the poet is possessed by a spirit not his own, and that he cannot poetize while he has a particle of understanding left. Again he says that the bacchantes, possessed by the god, drink milk and honey from the rivers, and cannot believe, *till they recover their senses*, that they have been drinking mere water. Empedocles said that "the mind could only conceive of fire by being fire."

All these definitions imply in the imaginative faculty the capabilities of ecstasy and possession, that is, of projecting itself into the very consciousness of its object, and again of being so wholly possessed by the emotion of its object that in expression it takes unconsciously the tone, the color, and the temperature thereof. Shakespeare is the highest example of this — for example, the parting of Romeo and Juliet. There the poet is so possessed by the situation, has so mingled his own consciousness with that of the lovers, that all nature is infected too, and is full of partings:

> Look, love, what envious streaks
> Do lace the *severing* clouds in yonder east.

In Shelley's "Cenci," on the other hand, we have an instance of the poet's imagination giving away its own consciousness to the object contemplated, in this case an inanimate one.

THE IMAGINATION

Two miles on this side of the fort, the road
Crosses a deep ravine; 't is rough and narrow,
And winds with short turns down the precipice;
And in its depth there is a mighty rock
Which has, from unimaginable years,
Sustained itself with terror and with toil
Over a gulf, and with the agony
With which it clings seems slowly coming down;
Even as a wretched soul hour after hour
Clings to the mass of life; yet clinging, leans;
And leaning, makes more dark the dread abyss
In which it fears to fall: beneath this crag,
Huge as despair, as if in weariness,
The melancholy mountain yawns.

The hint of this Shelley took from a passage in
the second act of Calderon's "Purgatorio de San
Patricio."

No ves ese peñasco que parece
Que se esta sustentando con trabajo,
Y con el ansia misma que padece
Ha tantos siglos que se viene abajo?

which, retaining the measure of the original, may
be thus paraphrased:

Do you not see that rock there which appeareth
To hold itself up with a throe appalling,
And, through the very pang of what it feareth,
So many ages hath been falling, falling?

You will observe that in the last instance quoted the
poet substitutes his own *impression* of the thing for
the thing itself; he forces his own consciousness upon
it, and herein is the very root of all sentimentalism.
Herein lies the fault of that subjective tendency
whose excess is so lamented by Goethe and Schiller,

[71]

and which is one of the main distinctions between ancient and modern poetry. I say in its excess, for there are moods of mind of which it is the natural and healthy expression. Thus Shakespeare in his ninety-seventh sonnet:

> How like a winter hath my absence been
> From thee, the pleasure of the fleeting year!
> What freezings have I felt, what dark days seen,
> What old December's bareness everywhere!
> And yet this time remov'd was summer's time.

It is only when it becomes a habit, instead of a mood of the mind, that it is a token of disease. Then it is properly dyspepsia, liver-complaint — what you will, but certainly not imagination as the handmaid of art. In that service she has two duties laid upon her: one as the *plastic* or *shaping* faculty, which gives form and proportion, and reduces the several parts of any work to an organic unity foreordained in that idea which is its germ of life; and the other as the *realizing* energy of thought which conceives clearly all the parts, not only in relation to the whole, but each in its several integrity and coherence.

We call the imagination the creative faculty. Assuming it to be so, in the one case it acts by deliberate forethought, in the other by intense sympathy — a sympathy which enables it to realize an Iago as happily as a Cordelia, a Caliban as a Prospero. There is a passage in Chaucer's "House

of Fame" which very prettily illustrates this latter
function:

> Whan any speche ycomen ys
> Up to the paleys, anon ryght
> Hyt wexeth lyke the same wight,
> Which that the worde in erthe spak,
> Be hyt clothed rede or blak;
> And so were hys lykenesse,
> And spake the word, that thou wilt gesse
> That it the same body be,
> Man or woman, he or she.

We have the highest, and indeed an almost unique,
example of this kind of sympathetic imagination in
Shakespeare, who becomes so sensitive, sometimes,
to the thought, the feeling, nay, the mere whim or
habit of body of his characters, that we feel, to use
his own words, as if "the dull substance of his flesh
were thought." It is not in mere intensity of phrase,
but in the fitness of it to the feeling, the character,
or the situation, that this phase of the imaginative
faculty gives witness of itself in expression. I know
nothing more profoundly imaginative therefore in its
bald simplicity than a line in Webster's "Duchess of
Malfy." Ferdinand has procured the murder of his
sister the duchess. When her dead body is shown to
him he stammers out:

> Cover her face; mine eyes dazzle; she died young.

The difference between subjective and objective
in poetry would seem to be that the aim of the former

is to express a mood of the mind, often something in itself accidental and transitory, while that of the latter is to convey the impression made upon the mind by something outside of it, but taken up into the mind and idealized (that is, stripped of all unessential particulars) by it. The one would fain set forth your view of the thing (modified, perhaps, by your breakfast), the other would set forth the very thing itself in its most concise individuality. Subjective poetry may be profound and imaginative if it deal with the primary emotions of our nature, with the soul's inquiries into its own being and doing, as was true of Wordsworth; but in the very proportion that it is profound, its range is limited. Great poetry should have breadth as well as height and depth; it should meet men everywhere on the open levels of their common humanity, and not merely on their occasional excursions to the heights of speculation or their exploring expeditions among the crypts of metaphysics.

But however we divide poetry, the office of imagination is to disengage what is essential from the crowd of accessories which is apt to confuse the vision of ordinary minds. For our perceptions of things are gregarious, and are wont to huddle together and jostle one another. It is only those who have been long trained to shepherd their thoughts that can at once single out each member of the flock by something peculiar to itself. That the power of abstraction has something to do with the imagination is clear, I think, from the fact that everybody is a dramatic poet (so far as the conception of character goes) in his sleep. His acquaintances walk and talk before him on the stage of dream precisely as in life. When he wakes, his genius has flown away with his sleep. It was indeed nothing more than that his mind was not distracted by the multiplicity of details which the senses force upon it by day. He thinks of Smith, and it is no longer a mere name on a doorplate or in a directory; but Smith himself is there, with those marvellous commonplaces of his which, could you only hit them off when you were awake, you would have created Justice Shallow. Nay, is not there, too, that offensively supercilious creak of the boots with which he enforced his remarks on the war in Europe, when he last caught you at the corner of the street and decanted into your ears the stale settlings of a week of newspapers? Now, did not Shakespeare tell us that the imagination *bodies forth?* It is indeed the *verbum caro factum* — the word made flesh and blood.

I said that the imagination always idealizes, that in its highest exercise, for example, as in the representation of character, it goes behind the species to the genus, presenting us with everlasting types of human nature, as in Don Quixote and Hamlet, Antigone and Cordelia, Alcestis and Amelia. By this I mean that those features are most constantly insisted upon, not in which they differ from other men, but from other kinds of men. For example, Don Quixote is never set before us as a mere madman, but as the victim of a monomania, and that, when you analyze it, of a very noble kind — nothing less, indeed, than devotion to an unattainable ideal, to an anachronism, as the ideals of imaginative men for the most part are. Amid all his ludicrous defeats and disillusions, this poetical side of him is brought to our notice at intervals, just as a certain theme recurs again and again in one of Beethoven's symphonies, a kind of clue to guide us through those intricacies of harmony. So in Lear, one of Shakespeare's profoundest psychological studies, the weakness of the man is emphasized, as it were, and forced upon our attention by his outbreaks of impotent violence; so in Macbeth, that imaginative bias which lays him open to the temptation of the weird sisters is suggested from time to time through the whole tragedy, and at last unmans him, and brings about his catastrophe in his combat with Macduff. This is what I call ideal and imaginative representation, which marks the outlines and boundaries of character, not by arbitrary lines drawn at this angle or that, according to the whim of the tracer, but by those mountain-ranges of human nature which divide man from man and temperament from temperament. And as the imagination of the reader must reinforce that of the poet, reducing the generic again to the specific, and defining it into sharper individuality by a comparison with the experiences of actual life, so, on the other hand, the popular imagination is always poetic, investing each new figure that comes before it with all the qualities that belong to the genus. Thus Hamlet, in some one or other of his characteristics has been the familiar of us all, and so from an ideal and remote figure is reduced to the standard of real and contemporary existence; while Bismarck, who, if we knew him, would probably turn out to be a comparatively simple character, is invested with all the qualities which have ever been attributed to the typical statesman, and is clearly as imaginative a personage as the Marquis of Posa, in Schiller's "Don Carlos." We are ready to accept any *coup de théâtre* of him. Now, this prepossession is precisely that for which the imagination of the poet makes us ready by working on our own.

But there are also lower levels on which this idealization plays its tricks upon our fancy. The Greek, who had studied profoundly what may be called the machinery of art, made use even of mechanical contrivances to delude the imagination of the spectator, and to entice him away from the associations of everyday life. The cothurnus lifted the actor to heroic stature, the mask prevented the ludicrous recognition of a familiar face in "Œdipus" and "Agamemnon"; it precluded grimace, and left the countenance as passionless as that of a god; it gave a more awful reverberation to the voice, and it was by the voice, that most penetrating and sympathetic, one might almost say incorporeal, organ of expression, that the great effects of the poet and tragic actor were wrought. Everything, you will observe, was, if not lifted above, at any rate removed, however much or little, from the plane of the actual and trivial. Their stage showed nothing that could be met in the streets. We barbarians, on the other hand, take delight precisely in that. We admire the novels of Trollope and the groups of Rogers because, as we say, they are so *real*, while it is only because they are so matter-of-fact, so exactly on the level with our own trivial and prosaic apprehensions. When Dante lingers to hear the dispute between Sinon and Master Adam, Virgil, type of the higher reason and the ideal poet, rebukes him, and even angrily.

> E fa ragion ch'io ti sia sempre allato
> Si più avvien che fortuna t' accoglia
> Ove sien genti in simigliante piato;
> Chè voler ciò udire è bassa voglia.

> Remember, *I* am always at thy side,
> If ever fortune bring thee once again
> Where there are people in dispute like this,
> For wishing to hear that is vulgar wish.

Verse is another of these expedients for producing
that frame of mind, that prepossession, on the part
of hearer or reader which is essential to the purpose
of the poet, who has lost much of his advantage by
the invention of printing, which obliges him to appeal
to the eye rather than the ear. The rhythm is no
arbitrary and artificial contrivance. It was suggested
by an instinct natural to man. It is taught him by
the beating of his heart, by his breathing, hastened
or retarded by the emotion of the moment. Nay, it
may be detected by what seems the most monoto-
nous of motions, the flow of water, in which, if you
listen intently, you will discover a beat as regular as
that of the metronome. With the natural presumption of all self-taught men, I thought I had made a
discovery in this secret confided to me by Beaver
Brook, till Professor Peirce told me it was always
allowed for in the building of dams. Nay, for my own
part, I would venture to affirm that not only metre
but even rhyme itself was not without suggestion in
outward nature. Look at the pine, how its branches,
balancing each other, ray out from the tapering stem
in stanza after stanza, how spray answers to spray
in order, strophe, and antistrophe, till the perfect
tree stands an embodied ode, Nature's triumphant
vindication of proportion, number, and harmony.
Who can doubt the innate charm of rhyme who has
seen the blue river repeat the blue o'erhead; who has

been ravished by the visible consonance of the tree growing at once toward an upward and downward heaven on the edge of the twilight cove; or who has watched how, as the kingfisher flitted from shore to shore, his visible echo flies under him, and completes the fleeting couplet in the visionary vault below? At least there can be no doubt that metre, by its systematic and regular occurrence, gradually subjugates and tunes the senses of the hearer, as the wood of the violin arranges itself in sympathy with the vibration of the strings, and thus that predisposition to the proper emotion is accomplished which is essential to the purpose of the pest. You must not only expect, but you must expect in the right way; you must be magnetized beforehand in every fibre by your own sensibility in order that you may feel what and how you ought. The right reception of whatever is ideally represented demands as a preliminary condition an exalted, or, if not that, then an excited, frame of mind both in poet and hearer. The imagination must be sensitized ere it will take the impression of those airy nothings whose image is traced and fixed by appliances as delicate as the golden pencils of the sun. Then that becomes a visible reality which before was but a phantom of the brain. Your own passion must penetrate and mingle with that of the artist that you may interpret him aright. You must, I say, be prepossessed, for it is the mind which shapes and colors the reports of the senses. Suppose you were expecting the bell to toll for the burial of some beloved person and the church-clock should begin to strike. The first lingering blow of the hammer would beat upon your very heart, and thence the shock would run to all the senses at once; but after a few strokes you would be undeceived, and the sound would become commonplace again. On the other hand, suppose that at a certain hour you knew that a criminal was to be executed; then the ordinary striking of the clock would have the sullen clang of a funeral bell. So in Shakespeare's instance of the lover, does he not suddenly find himself sensible of a beauty in the world about him before undreamed of, because his passion has somehow got into whatever he sees and hears? Will not the rustle of silk across a counter stop his pulse because it brings back to his sense the odorous whisper of Parthenissa's robe? Is not the beat of the horse's hoofs as rapid to Angelica pursued as the throbs of her own heart huddling upon one another in terror, while it is slow to Sister Anne, as the pulse that pauses between hope and fear, as she listens on the tower for rescue, and would have the rider "spur, though mounted on the wind"?

Dr. Johnson tells us that that only is good poetry which may be translated into sensible prose. I greatly doubt whether any very profound emotion can be so rendered. Man is a metrical animal, and it is not in prose but in nonsense verses that the young mother croons her joy over the new centre of hope and terror that is sucking life from her breast. Translate passion into sensible prose and it becomes absurd, because subdued to workaday associations, to that level of common sense and convention where to betray intense feeling is ridiculous and unmannerly. Shall I ask Shakespeare to translate me his love "still climbing trees in the Hesperides"? Shall I ask Marlowe how Helen could "make him immortal with a kiss," or how, in the name of all the Monsieur Jourdains, at once her face could "launch a thousand ships and burn the topless towers of Ilion"? Could Æschylus, if put upon the stand, defend his making Prometheus cry out,

> O divine ether and swift-winged winds,
> Ye springs of rivers, and of ocean waves
> The innumerable smile, all mother Earth,
> And Helios' all-beholding round, I call:
> Behold what I, a god, from gods endure!

Or could Lear justify his

> I tax not you, you elements, with unkindness;
> I never gave you kingdoms, call'd you children!

No; precisely what makes the charm of poetry is what we cannot explain any more than we can describe a perfume. There is a little quatrain of Gongora's quoted by Calderon in his "Alcalde of Zalamea" which has an inexplicable charm for me:

THE IMAGINATION

Las flores del romero,
    Niña Isabel,
Hoy son flores azules,
    Y mañana serán miel.

If I translate it, 't is nonsense, yet I understand it
perfectly, and it will, I dare say, outlive much wiser
things in my memory. It is the very function of
poetry to free us from that witch's circle of common
sense which holds us fast in its narrow enchantment.
In this disenthralment, language and verse have
their share, and we may say that language also is
capable of a certain idealization. Here is a passage
from the XXXth song of Drayton's "Poly-Olbion":

Which Copland scarce had spoke, but quickly every Hill
Upon her verge that stands, the neighbouring valleys fill;
Helvillon from his height, it through the mountains threw,
From whom as soon again, the sound Dunbalrase drew,
From whose stone-trophied head, it on to Wendrosse went,
Which tow'rds the sea again, resounded it to Dent,
That Broadwater therewith within her banks astound,
In sailing to the sea, told it in Egremound.

This gave a hint to Wordsworth, who, in one of his
"Poems on the Naming of Places," thus prolongs
the echo of it:

Joanna, looking in my eyes, beheld
That ravishment of mine, and laughed aloud.
The Rock, like something starting from a sleep,
Took up the Lady's voice, and laughed again;
The ancient Woman seated on Helm-crag
Was ready with her cavern; Hammar-scar,
And the tall steep of Silver-how, sent forth
A noise of laughter; southern Loughrigg heard,
And Fairfield answered with a mountain tone;

[83]

> Helvellyn far into the clear blue sky
> Carried the Lady's voice, — old Skiddaw blew
> His speaking-trumpet; — back out of the clouds
> Of Glaramara southward came the voice;
> And Kirkstone tossed it from his misty head.

Now, this passage of Wordsworth I should call the idealization of that of Drayton, who becomes poetical only in the "stone-trophied head of Dunbalrase"; and yet the thought of both poets is the same.

Even what is essentially vulgar may be idealized by seizing and dwelling on the generic characteristics. In "Antony and Cleopatra" Shakespeare makes Lepidus tipsy, and nothing can be droller than the drunken gravity with which he persists in proving himself capable of bearing his part in the conversation. We seem to feel the whirl in his head when we find his mind revolving round a certain fixed point to which he clings as to a post. Antony is telling stories of Egypt to Octavius, and Lepidus, drawn into an eddy of the talk, interrupts him:

Lepidus: You gave strange serpents there.
Antony [*trying to shake him off*]: Ay, Lepidus.
Lepidus: Your serpent of Egypt is bred now of your mud by the operation of your sun: so is your crocodile.
Antony [*thinking to get rid of him*]: They are so.

Presently Lepidus has revolved again, and continues, as if he had been contradicted:

Nay, certainly, I have heard the Ptolemies' pyramises are very goodly things; without contradiction, I have heard that.

And then, after another pause, still intent on proving himself sober, he asks, coming round to the crocodile again:

What manner o' thing is your crocodile?

Antony answers gravely:

It is shaped, sir, like itself, and it is as broad as it hath breadth; it is just so high as it is, and moves with its own organs: it lives by that which nourisheth it; and the elements once out of it, it transmigrates.

Lepidus: What color is it of?
Antony: Of its own color, too.
Lepidus [meditatively]: 'T is a strange serpent.

The ideal in expression, then, deals also with the generic, and evades embarrassing particulars in a generalization. We say Tragedy with the dagger and bowl, and it means something very different to the æsthetic sense from Tragedy with the case-knife and the phial of laudanum, though these would be as effectual for murder. It was a misconception of this that led poetry into that slough of poetic diction where everything was supposed to be made poetical by being called something else, and something longer. A boot became "the shining leather that the leg encased"; coffee, "the fragrant juice of Mocha's berry brown," whereas the imaginative way is the most condensed and shortest, conveying to the mind a feeling of the thing, and not a paraphrase of it. Akin to this was a confounding of the pictorial with the imaginative, and personification with that typical expression which is the true function of poetry. Compare, for example, Collins's Revenge with Chaucer's.

> Revenge impatient rose;
> He threw his blood-stained sword in thunder down,
> And, with a withering look,
> The war-denouncing trumpet took,
> And blew a blast so loud and dread,
> Were ne'er prophetic sound so full of woe!
> And ever and anon he beat
> The doubling drum with furious heat.

"Words, words, Horatio!" Now let us hear Chaucer with his single stealthy line that makes us glance over our shoulder as if we heard the murderous tread behind us:

> The smiler with the knife hid under the cloak.

Which is the more terrible? Which has more danger in it — Collins's noise or Chaucer's silence? Here is not the mere difference, you will perceive, between ornament and simplicity, but between a diffuseness which distracts, and a condensation which concentres the attention. Chaucer has chosen out of all the rest the treachery and the secrecy as the two points most apt to impress the imagination.

The imagination, as concerns expression, condenses; the fancy, on the other hand, adorns, illustrates, and commonly amplifies. The one is suggestive, the other picturesque. In Chapman's "Hero and Leander," I read —

> Her fresh-heat blood cast figures in her eyes,
> And she supposed she saw in Neptune's skies
> How her star wander'd, wash'd in smarting brine,
> For her love's sake, that with immortal wine
> Should be embathed, and swim in more heart's-ease
> Than there was water in the Sestian seas.

In the epithet "star," Hero's thought implies the beauty and brightness of her lover and his being the lord of her destiny, while in "Neptune's skies" we have not only the simple fact that the waters are the atmosphere of the sea-god's realm, but are reminded of that reflected heaven which Hero must have so often watched as it deepened below her tower in the smooth Hellespont. I call this as high an example of fancy as could well be found; it is picture and sentiment combined — the very essence of the picturesque.

But when Keats calls Mercury "the star of Lethe," the word " star " makes us see him as the poor ghosts do who are awaiting his convoy, while the word "Lethe" intensifies our sympathy by making us feel his coming as they do who are longing to drink of forgetfulness. And this again reacts upon the word "star," which, as it before expressed only the shining of the god, acquires a metaphysical significance from our habitual association of star with the notions of hope and promise. Again nothing can be more fanciful than this bit of Henry More the Platonist:

> What doth move
> The nightingale to sing so fresh and clear?
> The thrush or lark that, mounting high above,
> Chants her shrill notes to heedless ears of corn
> Heavily hanging in the dewy morn?

But compare this with Keats again:

> The voice I hear this passing night was heard
> In ancient days by emperor and clown;
> Perhaps the self-same song that found a path
> Through the sad heart of Ruth when, sick for home,
> She stood in tears amid the alien corn.

The imagination has touched that word "alien," and we see the field through Ruth's eyes, as she looked round on the hostile spikes, not merely through those of the poet.

CRITICAL FRAGMENTS

I. LIFE IN LITERATURE AND LANGUAGE

IT is the office and function of the imagination to renew life in lights and sounds and emotions that are outworn and familiar. It calls the soul back once more under the dead ribs of nature, and makes the meanest bush burn again, as it did to Moses, with the visible presence of God. And it works the same miracle for language. The word it has touched retains the warmth of life forever. We talk about the age of superstition and fable as if they were passed away, as if no ghost could walk in the pure white light of science, yet the microscope that can distinguish between the disks that float in the blood of man and ox is helpless, a mere dead eyeball, before this mystery of Being, this wonder of Life, the sympathy which puts us in relation with all nature, before that mighty circulation of Deity in which stars and systems are but as the blood-disks in our own veins. And so long as wonder lasts, so long will imagination find thread for her loom, and sit like the Lady of Shalott weaving that magical web in which "the shows of things are accommodated to the desires of the mind."

It is precisely before this phenomenon of life in

literature and language that criticism is forced to stop short. That it is there we know, but what it is we cannot precisely tell. It flits before us like the bird in the old story. When we think to grasp it, we already hear it singing just beyond us. It is the imagination which enables the poet to give away his own consciousness in dramatic poetry to his characters, in narrative to his language, so that they react upon us with the same original force as if they had life in themselves.

II. STYLE AND MANNER

WHERE Milton's style is fine it is *very* fine, but it is always liable to the danger of degenerating into mannerism. Nay, where the imagination is absent and the artifice remains, as in some of the theological discussions in "Paradise Lost," it becomes mannerism of the most wearisome kind. Accordingly, he is easily parodied and easily imitated. Philips, in his "Splendid Shilling," has caught the trick exactly:

> Not blacker tube nor of a shorter size
> Smokes Cambrobriton (versed in pedigree,
> Sprung from Cadwallader and Arthur, kings
> Full famous in romantic tale) when he,
> O'er many a craggy hill and barren cliff,
> Upon a cargo of famed Cestrian cheese
> High overshadowing rides, with a design
> To vend his wares or at the Arvonian mart,
> Or Maridunum, or the ancient town
> Yclept Brechinia, or where Vaga's stream
> Encircles Ariconium, fruitful soil.

Philips has caught, I say, Milton's trick; his real secret he could never divine, for where Milton is best, he is incomparable. But all authors in whom imagination is a secondary quality, and whose merit lies less in what they say than in the way they say it, are apt to become mannerists, and to have imitators, because manner can be easily imitated. Milton has more or less colored all blank verse since his time, and, as those who imitate never fail to exaggerate, his influence has in some respects been mischievous. Thomson was well-nigh ruined by him. In him a leaf cannot fall without a Latinism, and there is circumlocution in the crow of a cock. Cowper was only saved by mixing equal proportions of Dryden in his verse, thus hitting upon a kind of cross between prose and poetry. In judging Milton, however, we should not forget that in verse the music makes a part of the meaning, and that no one before or since has been able to give to simple pentameters the majesty and compass of the organ. He was as much composer as poet.

How is it with Shakespeare? did he have no style? I think I find the proof that he had it, and that of the very highest and subtlest kind, in the fact that I can nowhere put my finger on it, and say it is here or there.[1]

[1] In his essay, "Shakespeare Once More" (*Works*, III, pp. 36–42), published in 1868, Mr. Lowell has treated of Shakespeare's

ON POETRY AND BELLES-LETTRES

I do not mean that things in themselves artificial
may not be highly agreeable. We learn by degrees
to take a pleasure in the mannerism of Gibbon and
Johnson. It is something like reading Latin as a
living language. But in both these cases the man is
only present by his thought. It is the force of that,
and only that, which distinguishes them from their
imitators, who easily possess themselves of everything else. But with Burke, who has true style, we
have a very different experience. If we *go* along with
Johnson or Gibbon, we are *carried* along by Burke.
Take the finest specimen of him, for example, "The
Letter to a Noble Lord." The sentences throb with
the very pulse of the writer. As he kindles, the phrase
glows and dilates, and we feel ourselves sharing in
that warmth and expansion. At last we no longer
read, we seem to hear him, so livingly is the whole
man in what he writes; and when the spell is over,
we can scarce believe that those dull types could
have held such ravishing discourse. And yet we are
told that when Burke spoke in Parliament he always
emptied the house.

I know very well what the charm of mere words
is. I know very well that our nerves of sensation
adapt themselves, as the wood of the violin is said
to do, to certain modulations, so that we receive

style in a passage of extraordinary felicity and depth of critical
judgment.

them with a readier sympathy at every repetition. This is a part of the sweet charm of the classics. We are pleased with things in Horace which we should not find especially enlivening in Mr. Tupper. Cowper, in one of his letters, after turning a clever sentence, says, "There! if that had been written in Latin seventeen centuries ago by Mr. Flaccus, you would have thought it rather neat." How fully any particular rhythm gets possession of us we can convince ourselves by our dissatisfaction with any emendation made by a contemporary poet in his verses. Posterity may think he has improved them, but we are jarred by any change in the old tune. Even without any habitual association, we cannot help recognizing a certain power over our fancy in mere words. In verse almost every ear is caught with the sweetness of alliteration. I remember a line in Thomson's "Castle of Indolence" which owes much of its fascination to three *m*'s, where he speaks of the Hebrid Isles

> Far placed amid the melancholy main.

I remember a passage in Prichard's "Races of Man" which had for me all the moving quality of a poem. It was something about the Arctic regions, and I could never read it without the same thrill. Dr. Prichard was certainly far from being an inspired or inspiring author, yet there was something in those words, or in their collocation, that affected me as only genius can. It was probably some dimly felt association, something like that strange power there is in certain odors, which, in themselves the most evanescent and impalpable of all impressions on the senses, have yet a wondrous magic in recalling, and making present to us, some forgotten experience.

Milton understood the secret of memory perfectly well, and his poems are full of those little pitfalls for the fancy. Whatever you have read, whether in the classics, or in mediæval romance, all is there to stir you with an emotion not always the less strong because indefinable. Gray makes use of the same artifice, and with the same success.

There is a charm in the arrangement of words also, and that not only in verse, but in prose. The finest prose is subject to the laws of metrical proportion. For example, in the song of Deborah and Barak: "Awake, awake, Deborah! Awake, awake, utter a song! Arise, Barak, and lead thy captivity captive, thou son of Abinoam!" Or again, "At her feet he bowed; he fell, he lay down; at her feet he bowed, he fell; where he bowed, there he fell down dead."

Setting aside, then, all charm of association, all the influence to which we are unconsciously subjected by melody, by harmony, or even by the mere sound of words, we may say that style is distinguished from manner by the author's power of projecting his own emotion into what he writes. The stylist is occupied with the impression which certain things have made upon him; the mannerist is wholly concerned with the impression he shall make on others.

III. KALEVALA

BUT there are also two kinds of imagination, or rather two ways in which imagination may display itself — as an active power or as a passive quality of the mind. The former reshapes the impressions it receives from nature to give them expression in more ideal forms; the latter reproduces them simply and freshly without any adulteration by conventional phrase, without any deliberate manipulation of them by the conscious fancy. Imagination as an active power concerns itself with expression, whether it be in giving that unity of form which we call art, or in that intenser phrase where word and thing leap together in a vivid flash of sympathy, so that we almost doubt whether the poet was conscious of his own magic, and whether we ourselves have not communicated the very charm we feel. A few such utterances have come down to us to which every generation adds some new significance out of its own store, till they do for the imagination what proverbs do for the understanding, and, passing into the common currency of speech, become the property of every man and no man. On the other hand, wonder, which is the raw material in which imagination finds food for her loom, is the property of primitive peoples and primitive poets. There is always here a certain intimacy with nature, and a consequent simplicity of phrases and images, that please us all the more as the artificial conditions remove us farther from it. When a man happens to be born with that happy combination of qualities which enables him to renew this simple and natural relation with the world about him, however little or however much, we call him a poet, and surrender ourselves gladly to his gracious and incommunicable gift. But the renewal of these conditions becomes with the advance of every generation in literary culture and social refinement more difficult. Ballads, for example, are never produced among cultivated people. Like the mayflower, they love the woods, and will not be naturalized in the garden. Now, the advantage of that primitive kind of poetry of which I was just speaking is that it finds its imaginative components ready made to its hand. But an illustration is worth more than any amount of discourse. Let me read you a few passages from a poem which grew up under the true conditions of natural and primitive literature — remoteness, primitiveness of manners, and dependence on native traditions. I mean the epic of Finland — Kalevala.[1]

---

[1] This translation is Mr. Lowell's, and, so far as I know, has not been printed. — C. E. NORTON.

CRITICAL FRAGMENTS

I am driven by my longing,
Of my thought I hear the summons
That to singing I betake me,
That I give myself to speaking,
That our race's lay I utter,
Song for ages handed downward.
Words upon my lips are melting,
And the eager tones escaping
Will my very tongue outhasten,
Will my teeth, despite me, open.

Golden friend, belovèd brother,
Dear one that grew up beside me,
Join thee with me now in singing,
Join thee with me now in speaking,
Since we here have come together,
Journeying by divers pathways;
Seldom do we come together,
One comes seldom to the other,
In the barren fields far-lying,
On the hard breast of the Northland.

Hand in hand together clasping,
Finger fast with finger clasping,
Gladly we our song will utter,
Of our lays will give the choicest —
So that friends may understand it,
And the kindly ones may hear it,
In their youth which now is waxing,
Climbing upward into manhood:
These our words of old tradition,
These our lays that we have borrowed
From the belt of Wainamoinen,
From the forge of Ilmarinen,
From the sword of Kaukomeli,
From the bow of Jonkahainen,
From the borders of the ice-fields,
From the plains of Kalevala.

ON POETRY AND BELLES-LETTRES

These my father sang before me,
As the axe's helve he fashioned;
These were taught me by my mother,
As she sat and twirled her spindle,
While I on the floor was lying,
At her feet, a child was rolling;
Never songs of Sampo failed her,
Magic songs of Lonhi never;
Sampo in her song grew agèd,
Lonhi with her magic vanished,
In her singing died Wipunen,
As I played, died Lunminkainen.
Other words there are a many,
Magic words that I have taught me,
Which I picked up from the pathway,
Which I gathered from the forest,
Which I snapped from wayside bushes,
Which I gleaned from slender grass-blades,
Which I found upon the foot-bridge,
When I wandered as a herd-boy,
As a child into the pastures,
To the meadows rich in honey,
To the sun-begoldened hilltops,
Following the black Maurikki
By the side of brindled Kimmo.

Lays the winter gave me also,
Song was given me by the rain-storm,
Other lays the wind-gusts blew me,
And the waves of ocean brought them;
Words I borrowed of the song-birds,
And wise sayings from the tree-tops.

Then into a skein I wound them,
Bound them fast into a bundle,
Laid upon my ledge the burthen,
Bore them with me to my dwelling,
On the garret beams I stored them,
In the great chest bound with copper.

CRITICAL FRAGMENTS

Long time in the cold they lay there,
Under lock and key a long time;
From the cold shall I forth bring them?
Bring my lays from out the frost there
'Neath this roof so wide-renownèd?
Here my song-chest shall I open,
Chest with runic lays o'errunning?
Shall I here untie my bundle,
And begin my skein unwinding?

. . . .

Now my lips at last must close them
And my tongue at last be fettered;
I must leave my lay unfinished,
And must cease from cheerful singing;
Even the horses must repose them
When all day they have been running;
Even the iron's self grows weary
Mowing down the summer grasses;
Even the water sinks to quiet
From its rushing in the river;
Even the fire seeks rest in ashes
That all night hath roared and crackled;
Wherefore should not music also,
Song itself, at last grow weary
After the long eve's contentment
And the fading of the twilight?
I have also heard say often,
Heard it many times repeated,
That the cataract swift-rushing
Not in one gush spends its waters,
And in like sort cunning singers
Do not spend their utmost secret,
Yea, to end betimes is better
Than to break the thread abruptly.

Ending, then, as I began them,
Closing thus and thus completing,
I fold up my pack of ballads,
Roll them closely in a bundle,

Lay them safely in the storeroom,
In the strong bone-castle's chamber,
That they never thence be stolen,
Never in all time be lost thence,
Though the castle's wall be broken,
Though the bones be rent asunder,
Though the teeth may be pried open,
And the tongue be set in motion.

How, then, were it sang I always
Till my songs grew poor and poorer,
Till the dells alone would hear me,
Only the deaf fir-trees listen?
Not in life is she, my mother,
She no longer is aboveground;
She, the golden, cannot hear me,
'T is the fir-trees now that hear me,
'T is the pine-tops understand me,
And the birch-crowns full of goodness,
And the ash-trees now that love me!
Small and weak my mother left me,
Like a lark upon the cliff-top,
Like a young thrush 'mid the flintstones
In the guardianship of strangers,
In the keeping of the stepdame.
She would drive the little orphan,
Drive the child with none to love him,
To the cold side of the chimney,
To the north side of the cottage,
Where the wind that felt no pity,
Bit the boy with none to shield him.
Larklike, then, I forth betook me,
Like a little bird to wander,
Silent, o'er the country straying
Yon and hither, full of sadness.
With the winds I made acquaintance
Felt the will of every tempest,
Learned of bitter frost to shiver,
Learned too well to weep of winter.

CRITICAL FRAGMENTS

Yet there be full many people
Who with evil voice assail me,
And with tongue of poison sting me,
Saying that my lips are skilless,
That the ways of song I know not,
Nor the ballad's pleasant turnings.
Ah, you should not, kindly people,
Therein seek a cause to blame me,
That, a child, I sang too often,
That, unfledged, I twittered only.
I have never had a teacher,
Never heard the speech of great men,
Never learned a word unhomely,
Nor fine phrases of the stranger.
Others to the school were going,
I alone at home must keep me,
Could not leave my mother's elbow,
In the wide world had her only;
In the house had I my schooling,
From the rafters of the chamber,
From the spindle of my mother,
From the axehelve of my father,
In the early days of childhood;
But for this it does not matter,
I have shown the way to singers,
Shown the way, and blazed the tree-bark,
Snapped the twigs, and marked the footpath;
Here shall be the way in future,
Here the track at last be opened
For the singers better-gifted,
For the songs more rich than mine are,
Of the youth that now are waxing,
In the good time that is coming!

Like Virgil's husbandman, our minstrel did not
know how well off he was to have been without
schooling. This, I think, every one feels at once to
be poetry that sings itself. It makes its own tune,

and the heart beats in time to its measure. By and by poets will begin to say, like Goethe, "I sing as the bird sings"; but this poet sings in that fashion without thinking of it or knowing it. And it is the very music of his race and country which speaks through him with such simple pathos. Finland is the mother, and Russia is the stepdame, and the listeners to the old national lays grow fewer every day. Before long the Fins will be writing songs in the manner of Heine, and dramas in imitation of "Faust." Doubtless the material of original poetry lies in all of us, but in proportion as the mind is conventionalized by literature, it is apt to look about it for models, instead of looking inward for that native force which makes models, but does not follow them. This rose of originality which we long for, this bloom of imagination whose perfume enchants us — we can seldom find it when it is near us, when it is part of our daily lives.

REVIEWS OF CONTEMPORARIES

HENRY JAMES

JAMES'S TALES AND SKETCHES [1]

WHOEVER takes an interest, whether of mere curiosity or of critical foreboding, in the product and tendency of our younger literature, must have had his attention awakened and detained by the writings of Mr. James. Whatever else they may be, they are not common, and have that air of good breeding which is the token of whatever is properly called literature. They are not the overflow of a shallow talent for improvisation too full of self to be contained, but show everywhere the marks of intelligent purpose and of the graceful ease that comes only of conscientious training. Undoubtedly there was a large capital of native endowment to start from — a mind of singular subtlety and refinement; a faculty of rapid observation, yet patient of rectifying afterthought; senses daintily alive to every æsthetic suggestion; and a frank enthusiasm, kept within due bounds by the double-consciousness of humor. But it is plain that Mr. James is fortunate enough to possess, or to be possessed by, that finer sixth sense which we call the artistic, and which controls, cor-

[1] *A Passionate Pilgrim, and Other Tales.* By Henry James, Jr. Boston: J. R. Osgood & Co.
Transatlantic Sketches. By the same author.

rects, and discontents. His felicities, therefore, are not due to a lucky turn of the dice, but to forethought and afterthought. Accordingly, he is capable of progress, and gives renewed evidence of it from time to time, while too many of our authors show premature marks of arrested development. They strike a happy vein of starting, perhaps, and keep on grubbing at it, with the rude helps of primitive mining, seemingly unaware that it is daily growing more and more slender. Even should it wholly vanish, they persist in the vain hope of recovering it further on, as if in literature two successes of precisely the same kind were possible Nay, most of them have hit upon no vein at all, but picked up a nugget rather, and persevere in raking the surface of things, if haply they may chance upon another. The moral of one of Hawthorne's stories is that there is no element of treasure-trove in success, but that true luck lies in the deep and assiduous cultivation of our own plot of ground, be it larger or smaller. For indeed the only estate of man that savors of the realty is in his mind. Mr. James seems to have arrived early at an understanding of this, and to have profited by the best modern appliances of self-culture. In conception and expression is he essentially an artist and not an irresponsible *trouvère*. If he allow himself an occasional carelessness, it is not from incaution, but because he knows perfectly well what he is about. He

[106]

is quite at home in the usages of the best literary
society. In his writing there is none of that hit-or-
miss playing at snapdragon with language, of that
clownish bearing-on in what should be the light
strokes, as if mere emphasis were meaning, and naturally none of the slovenliness that offends a trained
judgment in the work of so many of our writers later,
unmistakably clever as they are. In short, he has
tone, the last result and surest evidence of an intellect
reclaimed from the rudeness of nature, for it means
self-restraint. The story of Handel's composing always in full dress conveys at least the useful lesson
of a gentlemanlike deference for the art a man pro-
fesses and for the public whose attention he claims.
Mr. James, as we see in his sketches of travel, is not
averse to the lounging ease of a shooting-jacket, but
he respects the usages of convention, and at the
canonical hours is sure to be found in the required
toilet. He does not expect the company to pardon
his own indolence as one of the necessary append-
ages of originality. Always considerate himself, his
readers soon find reason to treat him with consideration. For they soon come to see that literature may
be light and at the same time thoughtful; that light-
ness, indeed, results much more surely from serious
study than from the neglect of it.

We have said that Mr. James was emphatically a
man of culture, and we are old-fashioned enough to

look upon him with the more interest as a specimen of exclusively *modern* culture. Of any classical training we have failed to detect the traces in him. His allusions, his citations, are in the strictest sense contemporary, and indicate, if we may trust our divination, a preference for French models, Balzac, De Musset, Feuillet, Taine, Gautier, Mérimée, Sainte-Beuve, especially the three latter. He emulates successfully their suavity, their urbanity, their clever knack of conveying a fuller meaning by innuendo than by direct bluntness of statement. If not the best school for substance, it is an admirable one for method, and for so much of style as is attainable by example. It is the same school in which the writers of what used to be called our classical period learned the superior efficacy of the French small-sword as compared with the English cudgel, and Mr. James shows the graceful suppleness of that excellent academy of fence in which a man distinguishes by effacing himself. He has the dexterous art of letting us feel the point of his individuality without making us obtrusively aware of his presence. We arrive at an intimate knowledge of his character by confidences that escape egotism by seeming to be made always in the interest of the reader. That we know all his tastes and prejudices appears rather a compliment to our penetration than a proof of indiscreetness on his part. If we were disposed to find any fault with

[108]

Mr. James's style, which is generally of conspicuous elegance, it would be for his occasional choice of a French word or phrase (like *bouder, se reconnaît, banal,* and the like), where our English, without being driven to search her coffers round, would furnish one quite as good and surer of coming home to the ordinary reader. We could grow as near surly with him as would be possible for us with a writer who so generally endears himself to our taste, when he foists upon us a disagreeable alien like *abandon* (used as a noun), as if it could show an honest baptismal certificate in the registers of Johnson or Webster. Perhaps Mr. James finds, or fancies, in such words a significance that escapes our obtuser sense, a sweetness, it may be, of early association, for he tells us somewhere that in his boyhood he was put to school in Geneva. In this way only can we account for his once slipping into the rusticism that "remembers of" a thing.

But beyond any advantage which he may have derived from an intelligent study of French models, it is plain that a much larger share of Mr. James's education has been acquired by travel and through the eyes of a thoughtful observer of men and things. He has seen more cities and manners of men than was possible in the slower days of Ulysses, and if with less gain of worldly wisdom, yet with an enlargement of his artistic apprehensiveness and scope

that is of far greater value to him. We do not mean
to imply that Mr. James lacks what is called knowledge of the world. On the contrary, he has a great
deal of it, but it has not in him degenerated into
worldliness, and a mellowing haze of imagination
ransoms the edges of things from the hardness of
over-near familiarity. He shows on analysis that rare
combination of qualities which results in a man of
the world, whose contact with it kindles instead of
dampening the ardor of his fancy. He is thus excellently fitted for the line he has chosen as a story-
teller who deals mainly with problems of character
and psychology which spring out of the artificial
complexities of society, and as a translator of the
impressions received from nature and art into language that often lacks only verse to make it poetry.
Mr. James does not see things with his eyes alone.
His vision is always modified by his imaginative
temperament. He is the last man we should consult
for statistics, but his sketches give us the very mar-
row of sensitive impression, and are positively better
than the actual pilgrimage. We are tolerably familiar
with the scenes he describes, but hardly knew before
how much we had to be grateful for. *Et ego in Arcadia*,
we murmur to ourselves as we read, but surely this
was not the name we found in our guide-book. It is
always *Dichtung und Wahrheit* (Goethe knew very
well what he was about when he gave precedence to

the giddier sister) — it is always fact seen through
imagination and transfigured by it. A single example
will best show what we mean. "It is partly, doubtless, because their mighty outlines are still unsoftened
that the aqueducts are so impressive. *They seem the
very source of the solitude in which they stand;* they
look like architectural spectres, and loom through
the light mists of their grassy desert, as you recede
along the line, with the same insubstantial vastness
as if they rose out of Egyptian sands." Such happy
touches are frequent in Mr. James's pages, like flecks
of sunshine that steal softened through every chance
crevice in the leaves, as where he calls the lark a
"disembodied voice," or says of an English country-
church that "it made a Sunday where it stood." A
light-fingered poet would find many a temptation in
his prose. But it is not merely our fancies that are
pleased. Mr. James tempts us into many byways of
serious and fruitful thought. Especially valuable and
helpful have we found his *obiter dicta* on the arts of
painting, sculpture, and architecture; for example,
when he says of the Tuscan palaces that "in their
large dependence on pure symmetry for beauty of
effect, [they] reproduce more than other modern
styles the simple nobleness of Greek architecture."
And we would note also what he says of the Albani
Antinoüs. It must be a nimble wit that can keep pace
with Mr. James's logic in his æsthetic criticism. It is

apt to spring airily over the middle term to the conclusion, leaving something in the likeness of a ditch across the path of our slower intelligences, which look about them and think twice before taking the leap. Courage! there are always fresh woods and pastures new on the other side. A curious reflection has more than once flashed upon our minds as we lingered with Mr. James over his complex and refined sensations: we mean the very striking contrast between the ancient and modern traveller. The former saw with his bodily eyes, and reported accordingly, catering for the curiosity of homely wits as to the outsides and appearances of things. Even Montaigne, habitually introspective as he was, sticks to the old method in his travels. The modern traveller, on the other hand, superseded by the guidebook, travels in himself, and records for us the scenery of his own mind as it is affected by change of sky and the various weather of temperament.

Mr. James, in his sketches, frankly acknowledges his preference of the Old World. Life — which here seems all drab to him, without due lights and shades of social contrast, without that indefinable suggestion of immemorial antiquity which has so large a share in picturesque impression — is there a dome of many-colored glass irradiating both senses and imagination. We shall not blame him too gravely for this, as if an American had not as good a right as

any ancient of them all to say, *Ubi libertas, ibi patria.*
It is no real paradox to affirm that a man's love of
his country may often be gauged by his disgust at it.
But we think it might fairly be argued against him
that the very absence of that distracting complexity
of associations might help to produce that solitude
which is the main feeder of imagination. Certainly,
Hawthorne, with whom no modern European can be
matched for the subtlety and power of this marvellous quality, is a strong case on the American side
of the question.

Mr. James's tales, if without any obvious moral,
are sure to have a clearly defined artistic purpose.
They are careful studies of character thrown into
dramatic action, and the undercurrent of motive is,
as it should be, not in the circumstances but in the
characters themselves. It is by delicate touches and
hints that his effects are produced. The reader is
called upon to do his share, and will find his reward
in it, for Mr. James, as we cannot too often insist, is
first and always an artist. Nowhere does he show his
fine instinct more to the purpose than in leaving the
tragic element of tales (dealing as they do with contemporary life, and that mainly in the drawing-room)
to take care of itself, and in confining the outward
expression of passion within the limits of a decorous
amenity. Those who must have their intellectual
gullets tingled with the fiery draught of coarse sensa-

tion must go elsewhere for their dram; but whoever is capable of the aroma of the more delicate vintages will find it here. In the volume before us "Madame de Mauves" will illustrate what we mean. There is no space for detailed analysis, even if that were ever adequate to give the true impression of stories so carefully worked out and depending so much for their effect on a gradual cumulation of particulars each in itself unemphatic. We have said that Mr. James shows promise as well as accomplishment, gaining always in mastery of his material. It is but a natural inference from this that his "Roderick Hudson" is the fullest and most finished proof of his power as a story-teller. Indeed, we may say frankly that it pleases us the more because the characters are drawn with a bolder hand and in more determined outline, for if Mr. James need any friendly caution, it is against over-delicacy of handling.

THE COURTSHIP OF MILES STANDISH

THE introduction and acclimatization of the *hexameter* upon English soil has been an affair of more than two centuries. The attempt was first systematically made during the reign of Elizabeth, but the metre remained a feeble exotic that scarcely burgeoned under glass. Gabriel Harvey, — a kind of Don Adriano de Armado, — whose chief claim to remembrance is, that he was the friend of Spenser, boasts that he was the first to whom the notion of transplantation occurred. In his "Foure Letters" (1592) he says, "If I never deserve anye better remembraunce, let mee rather be Epitaphed, the Inventour of the English Hexameter, whome learned M. Stanihurst imitated in his Virgill, and excellent Sir Phillip Sidney disdained not to follow in his Arcadia and elsewhere." This claim of invention, however, seems to have been an afterthought with Harvey, for, in the letters which passed between him and Spenser in 1579, he speaks of himself more modestly as only a collaborator with Sidney and others in the good work. The Earl of Surrey is said to have been the first who wrote thus in English. The most successful person, however, was William Webb, who translated two of Virgil's Eclogues with a good deal of spirit and harmony. Ascham, in his "Schoolmaster" (1570), had already suggested the adoption of the ancient hexameter by English poets; but Ascham (as afterwards Puttenham in his "Art of Poesie") thought the ·number of monosyllabic words in English an insuperable objection to verses in which there was a large proportion of dactyls, and recommended, therefore, that a trial should be made with iambics. Spenser, at Harvey's instance, seems to have tried his hand at the new kind of verse. He says:

I like your late Englishe Hexameters so exceedingly well, that I also enure my penne sometimes in that kinde. . . . For the onely or chiefest hardnesse, whych seemeth, is in the Accente, which sometime gapeth, and, as it were, yawneth ilfauouredly, coming shorte of that it should, and sometime exceeding the measure of the Number, as in *Carpenter;* the middle sillable being vsed shorte in Speache, when it shall be read long in Verse, seemeth like a lame Gosling that draweth one legge after hir and *Heaven*, being used shorte as one sillable, when it is in Verse stretched out with a *Diastole*, is like a lame dogge that holdes up one legge. But it is to be wonne with Custome, and rough words must be subdued with Vse. For why a God's name may not we, as else the Greekes, have the kingdome of our owne Language, and measure our Accentes by the Sounde, reserving the Quantitie to the Verse?

The amiable Edmonde seems to be smiling in his sleeve as he writes this sentence. He instinctively saw the absurdity of attempting to subdue English to misunderstood laws of Latin quantities, which would, for example, make the vowel in "debt" long, in the teeth of use and wont.

We give a specimen of the hexameters which satisfied so entirely the ear of Master Gabriel Harvey, — an ear that must have been long by position, in virtue of its place on his head.

Not the like *Discourser*, for Tongue and head to be fóund out;
Not the like *resolute Man*, for great and serious áffayres;
Not the like *Lynx*, to spie out secretes and priuities óf States;
Eyed like to *Argus*, *Earde* like to *Midas*, *Nosd* like to *Naso*,
Winged like to *Mercury*, fittst of a Thousand for to be émployed.

And here are a few from "worthy M. Stanyhurst's" translation of the "Æneid."

Laocoon storming from Princelie Castel is hastning,
And a far of beloing: What fond phantastical harebraine
Madnesse hath enchaunted your wits, you townsmen unhappie?
Weene you (blind hodipecks) the Greekish nauie returned,
Or that their presents want craft? is subtil Vlisses
So soone forgotten? My life for an haulfpennie (Trojans), etc.

Mr. Abraham Fraunce translates two verses of Heliodorus thus: —

Now had fyery Phlegon his dayes reuolution ended,
And his snoring snowt with salt waues all to bee washed.

Witty Tom Nash was right enough when he called this kind of stuff, "that drunken, staggering kinde of verse which is all vp hill and downe hill, like the waye betwixt Stamford and Beechfeeld, and goes like a horse plunging through the myre in the deep of winter, now soust up to the saddle, and straight aloft on his tiptoes." It will be noticed that his prose falls into a kind of tipsy hexameter. The attempt in England at that time failed, but the controversy to which it gave rise was so far useful that it called forth Samuel Daniel's "Defence of Ryme" (1603), one of the noblest pieces of prose in the language. Hall also, in his "Satires," condemned the heresy in some verses remarkable for their grave beauty and strength.

The revival of the hexameter in modern poetry is due to Johann Heinrich Voss, a man of genius, an admirable metrist, and, Schlegel's sneer to the contrary notwithstanding, hitherto the best translator of Homer. His "Odyssey" (1783), his "Iliad" (1791), and his "Luise" (1795), were confessedly Goethe's teachers in this kind of verse. The "Hermann and Dorothea" of the latter (1798) was the first true poem written in modern hexameters. From Germany, Southey imported that and other classic metres into England, and we should be grateful to him, at least, for having given the model for Canning's "Knifegrinder." The exotic, however, again refused to take root, and for many years after we have no example of English hexameters. It was universally conceded that the temper of our language was unfriendly to them.

It remained for a man of true poetic genius to make them not only tolerated, but popular. Longfellow's translation of "The Children of the Lord's Supper" may have softened prejudice somewhat, but "Evan-

[118]

geline" (1847), though encumbered with too many
descriptive irrelevancies, was so full of beauty,
pathos, and melody, that it made converts by thou-
sands to the hitherto ridiculed measure. More than
this, it made Longfellow at once the most popular of
contemporary English poets. Clough's "Bothie" —
a poem whose singular merit has hitherto failed of the
wide appreciation it deserves — followed not long
after; and Kingsley's "Andromeda" is yet damp
from the press.

While we acknowledge that the victory thus won
by "Evangeline" is a striking proof of the genius of
the author, we confess that we have never been able
to overcome the feeling that the new metre is a dangerous and deceitful one. It is too easy to write, and
too uniform for true pleasure in reading. Its ease
sometimes leads Mr. Longfellow into prose, — as in
the verse

Combed and wattled gules and all the rest of the blazon,

and into a prosaic phraseology which has now and
then infected his style in other metres, as where he
says

Spectral gleam their snow-white *dresses*,

using a word as essentially unpoetic as "surtout or
pea-jacket." We think one great danger of the hexameter is, that it gradually accustoms the poet to be
content with a certain regular recurrence of accented

[119   ]

sounds, to the neglect of the poetic value of language and intensity of phrase.

But while we frankly avow our infidelity as regards the metre, we as frankly confess our admiration of the high qualities of "Miles Standish." In construction we think it superior to "Evangeline"; the narrative is more straightforward, and the characters are defined with a firmer touch. It is a poem of wonderful picturesqueness, tenderness, and simplicity, and the situations are all conceived with the truest artistic feeling. Nothing can be better, to our thinking, than the picture of Standish and Alden in the opening scene, tinged as it is with a delicate humor, which the contrast between the thoughts and characters of the two heightens almost to pathos. The pictures of Priscilla spinning, and the bridal procession, are also masterly. We feel charmed to see such exquisite imaginations conjured out of the little old familiar anecdote of John Alden's vicarious wooing. We are astonished, like the fisherman in the Arabian tale, that so much genius could be contained in so small and leaden a casket. Those who cannot associate sentiment with the fair Priscilla's maiden name of Mullins may be consoled by hearing that it is only a corruption of the Huguenot Desmoulins — as Barnum is of the Norman Vernon.

Indifferent poets comfort themselves with the notion that contemporary popularity is no test of merit, and that true poetry must always wait for a new generation to do it justice. The theory is not true in any general sense. With hardly an exception, the poetry that was ever to receive a wide appreciation has received it at once. Popularity in itself is no test of permanent literary fame, but the kind of it is and always has been a very decided one. Mr. Longfellow has been greatly popular because he so greatly deserved it. He has the secret of all the great poets — the power of expressing universal sentiments simply and naturally. A false standard of criticism has obtained of late, which brings a brick as a sample of the house, a line or two of condensed expression as a gauge of the poem. But it is only the whole poem that is a proof of the poem, and there are twenty fragmentary poets, for one who is capable of simple and sustained beauty. Of this quality Mr. Longfellow has given repeated and striking examples, and those critics are strangely mistaken who think that what he does is easy to be done, because he has the power to make it seem so. We think his chief fault is a too great tendency to moralize, or rather, a distrust of his readers, which leads him to point out the moral which he wishes to be drawn from any special poem. We wish, for example, that the last two stanzas could be cut off from "The Two Angels," a poem which, without them, is as perfect as anything in the language.

Many of the pieces in this volume having already

shone as captain jewels in Maga's carcanet, need no comment from us; and we should, perhaps, have avoided the delicate responsibility of criticizing one of our most precious contributors, had it not been that we have seen some very unfair attempts to depreciate Mr. Longfellow, and that, as it seemed to us, for qualities which stamp him as a true and original poet. The writer who appeals to more peculiar moods of mind, to more complex or more esoteric motives of emotion, may be a greater favorite with the few; but he whose verse is in sympathy with moods that are human and not personal, with emotions that do not belong to periods in the development of individual minds, but to all men in all years, wins the gratitude and love of whoever can read the language which he makes musical with solace and aspiration. The present volume, while it will confirm Mr. Longfellow's claim to the high rank he has won among lyric poets, deserves attention also as proving him to possess that faculty of epic narration which is rarer than all others in the nineteenth century. In our love of stimulants, and our numbness of taste, which craves the red pepper of a biting vocabulary, we of the present generation are apt to overlook this almost obsolete and unobtrusive quality; but we doubt if, since Chaucer, we have had an example of more purely objective narrative than in "The Courtship of Miles Standish." Apart from its intrinsic beauty, this

gives the poem a claim to higher and more thoughtful consideration; and we feel sure that posterity will
confirm the verdict of the present in regard to a poet
whose reputation is due to no fleeting fancy, but to
an instinctive recognition by the public of that which
charms now and charms always, — true power and
originality, without grimace and distortion; for
Apollo, and not Milo, is the artistic type of strength.

TALES OF A WAYSIDE INN

It is no wonder that Mr. Longfellow should be the
most popular of American, we might say, of contemporary poets. The fine humanity of his nature, the
wise simplicity of his thought, the picturesqueness of
his images, and the deliciously limpid flow of his
style, entirely justify the public verdict, and give as-
surance that his present reputation will settle into
fame. That he has not *this* of Tennyson, nor *that* of
Browning, may be cheerfully admitted, while he has
so many other things that are his own. There may be
none of those flashes of lightning in his verse that
make day for a moment in this dim cavern of consciousness where we grope; but there is an equable
sunshine that touches the landscape of life with a
new charm, and lures us out into healthier air. If he
fall short of the highest reaches of imagination, he is
none the less a master within his own sphere — all
the more so, indeed, that he is conscious of his own

[123   ]

limitations, and wastes no strength in striving to be other than himself. Genial, natural, and original, as much as in these latter days it is given to be, he holds a place among our poets like that of Irving among our prose-writers. Make whatever deductions and qualifications, and they still keep their place in the hearts and minds of men. In point of time he is our Chaucer — the first who imported a finer foreign culture into our poetry.

His present volume shows a greater ripeness than any of its predecessors. We find a mellowness of early autumn in it. There is the old sweetness native to the man, with greater variety of character and experience. The personages are all drawn from the life, and sketched with the light firmness of a practised art. They have no more individuality than is necessary to the purpose of the poem, which consists of a series of narratives told by a party of travellers gathered in Sudbury Inn, and each suited, either by its scene or its sentiment, to the speaker who recites it. In this also there is a natural reminiscence of Chaucer; and if we miss the rich minuteness of his Van Eyck painting, or the depth of his thoughtful humor, we find the same airy grace, tenderness, simple strength, and exquisite felicities of description. Nor are twinkles of sly humor wanting. The Interludes, and above all the Prelude, are masterly examples of that perfect ease of style which is, of all things, the hardest to attain. The verse flows clear and sweet as honey, and with a faint fragrance that tells, but not too plainly, of flowers that grew in many fields. We are made to feel that, however tedious the processes of culture may be, the ripe result in facile power and scope of fancy is purely delightful. We confess that we are so heartily weary of those cataclysms of passion and sentiment with which literature has been convulsed of late, — as if the main object were, not to move the reader, but to shake the house about his ears, — that the homelike quiet and beauty of such poems as these is like an escape from noise to nature.

As regards the structure of the work looked at as a whole, it strikes us as a decided fault, that the Saga of King Olaf is so disproportionately long, especially as many of the pieces which compose it are by no means so well done as the more strictly original ones. We have no quarrel with the foreign nature of the subject as such, — for any good matter is American enough for a truly American poet; but we cannot help thinking that Mr. Longfellow has sometimes mistaken mere strangeness for freshness, and has failed to make his readers feel the charm he himself felt. Put into English, the Saga seems *too* Norse; and there is often a hitchiness in the verse that suggests translation with overmuch heed for literal closeness. It is possible to assume alien forms of verse, but hardly to enter into forms of thought alien both in time and in the ethics from which they are derived. "The Building of the Long Serpent" is not to be named with Mr. Longfellow's "Building of the Ship," which he learned from no Heimskringla, but from the dockyards of Portland, where he played as a boy. We are willing, however, to pardon the parts which we find somewhat ineffectual, in favor of the "Nun of Nidaros," which concludes, and in its gracious piety more than redeems, them all.

WHITTIER

IN WAR TIME, AND OTHER POEMS

IT is a curious illustration of the attraction of opposites, that, among our elder poets, the war we are waging finds its keenest expression in the Quaker Whittier. Here is, indeed, a soldier prisoner on parole in a drab coat, with no hope of exchange, but with a heart beating time to the tap of the drum. Mr. Whittier is, on the whole, the most American of our poets, and there is a fire of warlike patriotism in him that burns all the more intensely that it is smothered by his creed. But it is not as a singular antithesis of dogma and character that this peculiarity of his is interesting to us. The fact has more significance as illustrating how deep an impress the fathers of New England stamped upon the commonwealth they founded. Here is a descendant and member of the sect they chiefly persecuted, more deeply imbued with the spirit of the Puritans than even their own lineal representatives. The New Englander is too strong for the sectarian, and the hereditary animosity softens to reverence, as the sincere man, looking back, conjures up the image of a sincerity as pure, though more stern, than his own. And yet the poetic sentiment of Whittier misleads him as far in admiration, as the pitiful snobbery of certain renegades perverts

[127]

them to depreciation, of the Puritans. It is not in any sense true that these pious and earnest men brought with them to the New World the deliberate fore-thought of the democracy which was to develop itself from their institutions. They brought over its seed, but unconsciously, and it was the kindly nature of the soil and climate that was to give it the chance to propagate and disperse itself. The same conditions have produced the same results also at the South, and nothing but slavery blocks the way to a perfect sympathy between the two sections.

Mr. Whittier is essentially a lyric poet, and the fervor of his temperament gives his pieces of that kind a remarkable force and effectiveness. Twenty years ago many of his poems were in the nature of *conciones ad populum*, vigorous stump-speeches in verse, appealing as much to the blood as the brain, and none the less convincing for that. By regular gradations ever since his tone has been softening and his range widening. As a poet he stands somewhere between Burns and Cowper, akin to the former in patriotic glow, and to the latter in intensity of reli-gious anxiety verging sometimes on morbidness. His humanity, if it lack the humorous breadth of the one, has all the tenderness of the other. In love of out-ward nature he yields to neither. His delight in it is not a new sentiment or a literary tradition, but the genuine passion of a man born and bred in the coun-

try, who has not merely a visiting acquaintance with
the landscape, but stands on terms of lifelong friendship with hill, stream, rock, and tree. In his descrip-
tions he often catches the *expression* of rural scenery,
a very different thing from the mere *looks*, with the
trained eye of familiar intimacy. A somewhat shy
and hermitical being we take him to be, and more
a student of his own heart than of men. His characters, where he introduces such, are commonly ab-
stractions, with little of the flesh and blood of real
life in them, and this from want of experience rather
than of sympathy; for many of his poems show him
capable of friendship almost womanly in its purity
and warmth. One quality which we especially value
in him is the intense home-feeling which, without any
conscious aim at being American, gives his poetry a
flavor of the soil surprisingly refreshing. Without being narrowly provincial, he is the most indigenous of
our poets. In these times, especially, his uncalculat-
ing love of country has a profound pathos in it. He
does not flare the flag in our faces, but one feels the
heart of a lover throbbing in his anxious verse.

Mr. Whittier, if the most fervid of our poets, is
sometimes hurried away by this very quality, in itself an excellence, into being the most careless. He
draws off his verse while the fermentation is yet going
on, and before it has had time to compose itself and
clarify into the ripe wine of expression. His rhymes

are often faulty beyond the most provincial license even of Burns himself. Vigor without elegance will never achieve permanent success in poetry. We think, also, that he has too often of late suffered himself to be seduced from the true path to which his nature set up finger-posts for him at every corner, into metaphysical labyrinths whose clue he is unable to grasp. The real life of his genius smoulders into what the woodmen call a *smudge*, and gives evidence of itself in smoke instead of flame. Where he follows his truer instincts, he is often admirable in the highest sense, and never without the interest of natural thought and feeling naturally expressed.

HOME BALLADS AND POEMS

THE natural product of a creed which ignores the æsthetical part of man and reduces Nature to a uniform drab would seem to have been Bernard Barton. *His* verse certainly infringed none of the superstitions of the sect; for from title-page to colophon there was no sin either in the way of music or color. There was, indeed, a frugal and housewifely Muse, that brewed a cup, neither cheering unduly nor inebriating, out of the emptyings of Wordsworth's teapot. How that little busy B. improved each shining hour, how neatly he laid his wax, it gives us a cold shiver to think of — *ancora ci raccappriccia!* Against a copy of verses signed "B. B.," as we remember them in the hardy Annuals that went to seed so many years ago, we should warn our incautious offspring as an experienced duck might her brood against a charge of B. B. shot. It behooves men to be careful; for one may chance to suffer lifelong from these intrusions of cold lead in early life, as duellists sometimes carry about all their days a bullet from which no surgery can relieve them. Memory avenges our abuses of her, and, as an awful example, we mention the fact that we have never been able to forget certain stanzas of another B. B., who, under the title of "Boston Bard," whilom obtained from newspaper columns that concession which gods and men would unanimously have denied him.

George Fox, utterly ignoring the immense stress which Nature lays on established order and precedent, got hold of a half-truth which made him crazy, as half-truths are wont. But the inward light, whatever else it might be, was surely not of that kind "that never was on land or sea." There has been much that was poetical in the lives of Quakers, little in the men themselves. Poetry demands a richer and more various culture, and, however good we may find such men as John Woolman and Elias Boudinot, they make us feel painfully that the salt of the earth is something very different, to say the least, from the Attic variety of the same mineral. Let Armstrong and Whitworth and James experiment as they will,

they shall never hit on a size of bore so precisely adequate for the waste of human life as the journal of an
average Quaker. Compared with it, the sandy intervals of Swedenborg gush with singing springs, and
Cotton Mather is a very Lucian for liveliness.

Yet this dry Quaker stem has fairly blossomed at
last, and Nature, who can never be long kept under,
has made a poet of Mr. Whittier as she made a General of Greene. To make a New England poet, she
had her choice between Puritan and Quaker, and she
took the Quaker. He is, on the whole, the most representative poet that New England has produced. He
sings her thoughts, her prejudices, her scenery. He
has not forgiven the Puritans for hanging two or
three of his co-sectaries, but he admires them for all
that, calls on his countrymen as

Sons of men who sat in council with their Bibles round the board,
Answering Charles's royal mandate with a stern "Thus saith the
Lord,"

and at heart, we suspect, has more sympathy with
Miles Standish than with Mary Dyer. Indeed,

Sons of men who sat in meeting with their broadbrims o'er their
brow,
Answering Charles's royal mandate with a *thee* instead of *thou*,

would hardly do. Whatever Mr. Whittier may lack,
he has the prime merit that he smacks of the soil.
It is a New England heart he buttons his straight-
breasted coat over, and it gives the buttons a sharp

[132]

strain now and then. Even the native idiom crops out here and there in his verses. He makes *abroad* rhyme with *God*, *law* with *war*, *us* with *curse*, *scorner* with *honor*, *been* with *men*, *beard* with *shared*. For the last two we have a certain sympathy as archaisms, but with the rest we can make no terms whatever, — they must march out with no honors of war. The Yankee lingo is insoluble in poetry, and the accent would give a flavor of *essence-pennyr'y'l* to the very Beatitudes. It differs from Lowland Scotch as a *patois* from a dialect.

But criticism is not a game of jerk-straws, and Mr. Whittier has other and better claims on us than as a stylist. There is true fire in the heart of the man, and his eye is the eye of a poet. A more juicy soil might have made him a Burns or a Béranger for us. New England is dry and hard, though she have a warm nook in her, here and there, where the magnolia grows after a fashion. It is all very nice to say to our poets, "You have sky and wood and waterfall and men and women — in short, the entire outfit of Shakespeare; Nature is the same here as elsewhere"; and when the popular lecturer says it, the popular audience gives a stir of approval. But it is all *bosh*, nevertheless. Nature is *not* the same here, and perhaps never will be, as in lands where man has mingled his being with hers for countless centuries, where every field is steeped in history, every crag is ivied with legend, and the whole atmosphere of thought is hazy with the Indian summer of tradition. Nature without an ideal background is nothing. We may claim whatever merits we like (and our orators are not too bashful), we may be as free and enlightened as we choose, but we are certainly not interesting or picturesque. We may be as beautiful to the statistician as a column of figures, and dear to the political economist as a social phenomenon; but our hive has little of that marvellous bee-bread that can transmute the brain to finer issues than a gregarious activity in hoarding. The Puritans left us a fine estate in conscience, energy, and respect for learning; but they disinherited us of the past. Not a single stage-property of poetry did they bring with them but the good old Devil, with his graminivorous attributes, and even he could not stand the climate. Neither horn nor hoof nor tail of him has been seen for a century. He is as dead as the goat-footed Pan, whom he succeeded, and we tenderly regret him.

Mr. Whittier himself complains somewhere of

The rigor of our frozen sky,

and he seems to have been thinking of our clear, thin, intellectual atmosphere, the counterpart of our physical one, of which artists complain that it rounds no edges. We have sometimes thought that his verses suffered from a New England taint in a too great

[134]

tendency to metaphysics and morals, which may be
the bases on which poetry rests, but should not be
carried too high above-ground. Without this, however, he would not have been the typical New England poet that he is. In the present volume there is
little of it. It is more purely objective than any of its
forerunners, and is full of the most charming rural
pictures and glimpses, in which every sight and
sound, every flower, bird, and tree, is neighborly and
homely. He makes us see

> the old swallow-haunted barns,
> Brown-gabled, long, and full of seams
> Through which the moted sunlight streams,
> And winds blow freshly in to shake
> The red plumes of the roosted cocks
> And the loose hay-mow's scented locks, —

> the cattle-yard
> With the white horns tossing above the wall,

the spring-blossoms that drooped over the river,

> Lighting up the swarming shad, —

and

> the bulged nets sweeping shoreward
> With their silver-sided haul.

Every picture is full of color, and shows that true
eye for Nature which sees only what it ought, and
that artistic memory which brings home composi-
tions and not catalogues. There is hardly a hill, rock,
stream, or sea-fronting headland in the neighborhood
of his home that he has not fondly remembered.

Sometimes, we think, there is too much description, the besetting sin of modern verse, which has substituted what should be called wordy-painting for the old art of painting in a single word. The essential character of Mr. Whittier's poetry is lyrical, and the rush of the lyric, like that of a brook, allows few pictures. Now and then there may be an eddy where the feeling lingers and reflects a bit of scenery, but for the most part it can only catch gleams of color that mingle with the prevailing tone and enrich without usurping on it. This volume contains some of the best of Mr. Whittier's productions in this kind. "Skipper Ireson's Ride " we hold to be by long odds the best of modern ballads. There are others nearly as good in their way, and all, with a single exception, embodying native legends. In "Telling the Bees," Mr. Whittier has enshrined a country superstition in a poem of exquisite grace and feeling. "The Garrison of Cape Ann" would have been a fine poem, but it has too much of the author in it, and to put a moral at the end of a ballad is like sticking a cork on the point of a sword. It is pleasant to see how much our Quaker is indebted for his themes to Cotton Mather, who belabored his un-Friends of former days with so much bad English and worse Latin. With all his faults, that conceited old pedant contrived to make one of the most entertaining books ever written on this side the water, and we wonder that no one should take the trouble to give us a tolerably correct edition of it. Absurdity is common enough, but such a genius for it as Mather had is a rare and delightful gift.

This last volume has given us a higher conception of Mr. Whittier's powers. We already valued as they deserved his force of faith, his earnestness, the glow and hurry of his thought, and the (if every third stump-speaker among us were not a Demosthenes, we should have said Demosthenean) eloquence of his verse; but here we meet him in a softer and more meditative mood. He seems a Berserker turned Carthusian. The half-mystic tone of "The Shadow and the Light" contrasts strangely, and, we think, pleasantly, with the warlike clang of "From Perugia." The years deal kindly with good men, and we find a clearer and richer quality in these verses where the ferment is over and the *rile* has quietly settled. We have had no more purely American poet than Mr. Whittier, none in whom the popular thought found such ready and vigorous expression. The future will not fail to do justice to a man who has been so true to the present.

SNOW-BOUND: A WINTER IDYL

At the close of his poem Mr. Whittier utters a hope that it may recall some pleasant country memories to the overworked slaves of our great cities, and that he may deserve those thanks which are all the more grateful that they are rather divined by the receiver than directly expressed by the giver. The reviewer cannot aspire to all the merit of this confidential privacy and pleasing shyness of gratitude, but he may fairly lay claim to a part of it, inasmuch as, though obliged to speak his thanks publicly, he need not do it to the author's face. We are again indebted to Mr. Whittier, as we have been so often before, for a very real and a very refined pleasure. The little volume before us has all his most characteristic merits. It is true to Nature and in local coloring, pure in sentiment, quietly deep in feeling, and full of those simple touches which show the poetic eye and the trained hand. Here is a New England interior glorified with something of that inward light which is apt to be rather warmer in the poet than the Quaker, but which, blending the qualities of both in Mr. Whittier, produces that kind of spiritual picturesqueness which gives so peculiar a charm to his verse. There is in this poem a warmth of affectionate memory and religious faith as touching as it is uncommon, and which would be altogether delightful if it did not remind us that the poet was growing old. Not that there is any other mark of senescence than the ripened sweetness of a life both publicly and privately well spent. There is fire enough, but it glows more equably and shines on sweeter scenes

than in the poet's earlier verse. It is as if a brand
from the camp-fire had kindled these logs on the old
homestead's hearth, whose flickering benediction
touches tremulously those dear heads of long ago
that are now transfigured with a holier light. The
father, the mother, the uncle, the schoolmaster, the
uncanny guest, are all painted in warm and natural
colors, with perfect truth of detail and yet with all
the tenderness of memory. Of the family group the
poet is the last on earth, and there is something
deeply touching in the pathetic sincerity of the
affection which has outlived them all, looking back
to before the parting, and forward to the assured
reunion.

But aside from its poetic and personal interest,
and the pleasure it must give to every one who loves
pictures from the life, "Snow-Bound" has something of historical interest. It describes scenes and
manners which the rapid changes of our national
habits will soon have made as remote from us as if
they were foreign or ancient. Already, alas! even in
farmhouses, backlog and forestick are obsolescent
words, and close-mouthed stoves chill the spirit while
they bake the flesh with their grim and undemon-
strative hospitality. Already are the railroads dis-
placing the companionable cheer of crackling walnut
with the dogged self-complacency and sullen virtue
of anthracite. Even where wood survives, he is too

often shut in the dreary madhouse cell of an airtight, round which one can no more fancy a social mug of flip circling than round a coffin. Let us be thankful that we can sit in Mr. Whittier's chimney-corner and believe that the blaze he has kindled for us shall still warm and cheer, when a wood fire is as faint a tradition in New as in Old England.

We have before had occasion to protest against Mr. Whittier's carelessness in accents and rhymes, as in pronouncing "ly'ceum," and joining in unhallowed matrimony such sounds as *awn* and *orn*, *ents* and *ence*. We would not have the Muse emulate the unidiomatic preciseness of a normal school-mistress, but we cannot help thinking that, if Mr. Whittier writes thus on principle, as we begin to suspect, he errs in forgetting that thought so refined as his can be fitly matched only with an equal refinement of expression, and loses something of its charm when cheated of it. We hope he will, at least, never mount Pega'sus, or water him in Heli'con, and that he will leave Mu'seum to the more vulgar sphere and obtuser sensibilities of Barnum. Where Nature has sent genius, she has a right to expect that it shall be treated with a certain elegance of hospitality.

POETRY AND NATIONALITY[1]

ONE of the dreams of our earlier horoscope-mongers was, that a poet should come out of the West, fashioned on a scale somewhat proportioned to our geographical pretensions. Our rivers, forests, mountains, cataracts, prairies, and inland seas were to find in him their antitype and voice. Shaggy he was to be, brown-fisted, careless of proprieties, unhampered by tradition, his Pegasus of the half-horse, half-alligator breed. By him at last the epos of the New World was to be fitly sung, the great tragi-comedy of democracy put upon the stage for all time. It was a cheap vision, for it cost no thought; and, like all judicious prophecy, it muffled itself from criticism in the loose drapery of its terms. Till the advent of this splendid apparition, who should dare affirm positively that he would never come? that, indeed, he was impossible? And yet his impossibility was demonstrable, nevertheless.

Supposing a great poet to be born in the West, though he would naturally levy upon what had al-

[1] This essay, to which I have given the above title, forms the greater part of a review of poems by John James Piatt. The brief, concluding portion of the review is of little value and is omitted here. Piatt died several years ago. He was a great friend of William Dean Howells, and once published a volume of poems in collaboration with him. A. M.

ways been familiar to his eyes for his images and illustrations, he would almost as certainly look for his ideal somewhere outside of the life that lay immediately about him. Life in its large sense, and not as it is temporarily modified by manners or politics, is the only subject of the poet; and though its elements lie always close at hand, yet in its unity it seems always infinitely distant, and the difference of angle at which it is seen in India and in Minnesota is almost inappreciable. Moreover, a rooted discontent seems always to underlie all great poetry, if it be not even the motive of it. The Iliad and the Odyssey paint manners that are only here and there incidentally true to the actual, but which in their larger truth had either never existed or had long since passed away. Had Dante's scope been narrowed to contemporary Italy, the "Divina Commedia" would have been a picture-book merely. But his theme was Man, and the vision that inspired him was of an Italy that never was nor could be, his political theories as abstract as those of Plato or Spinoza. Shakespeare shows us less of the England that then was than any other considerable poet of his time. The struggle of Goethe's whole life was to emancipate himself from Germany, and fill his lungs for once with a more universal air.

Yet there is always a flavor of the climate in these rare fruits, some gift of the sun peculiar to the region that ripened them. If we are ever to have a national poet, let us hope that his nationality will be of this subtle essence, something that shall make him unspeakably nearer to us, while it does not provincialize him for the rest of mankind. The popular recipe for compounding him would give us, perhaps, the most sublimely furnished bore in human annals. The novel aspects of life under our novel conditions may give some freshness of color to our literature; but democracy itself, which many seem to regard as the necessary Lucina of some new poetic birth, is altogether too abstract an influence to serve for any such purpose. If any American author may be looked on as in some sort the result of our social and political ideal, it is Emerson, who, in his emancipation from the traditional, in the irresponsible freedom of his speculation, and his faith in the absolute value of his own individuality, is certainly, to some extent, typical; but if ever author was inspired by the past, it is he, and he is as far as possible from the shaggy hero of prophecy. Of the sham-shaggy, who have tried the trick of Jacob upon us, we have had quite enough, and may safely doubt whether this satyr of masquerade is to be our representative singer.[1] Were it so, it would not be greatly to the credit of democracy as

[1] This is undoubtedly an allusion to Walt Whitman, who is mentioned by name, also derogatorily, in the next essay on Howells. The Howells essay appeared two years before the above. A. M.

an element of æsthetics. But we may safely hope for better things.

The themes of poetry have been pretty much the same from the first; and if a man should ever be born among us with a great imagination, and the gift of the right word, — for it is these, and not sublime spaces, that make a poet, — he will be original rather in spite of democracy than in consequence of it, and will owe his inspiration quite as much to the accumulations of the Old World as to the promises of the New. But for a long while yet the proper conditions will be wanting, not, perhaps, for the birth of such a man, but for his development and culture. At present, with the largest reading population in the world, perhaps no country ever offered less encouragement to the higher forms of art or the more thorough achievements of scholarship. Even were it not so, it would be idle to expect us to produce any literature so peculiarly our own as was the natural growth of ages less communicative, less open to every breath of foreign influence. Literature tends more and more to become a vast commonwealth, with no dividing lines of nationality. Any more Cids, or Songs of Roland, or Nibelungens, or Kalewalas are out of the question, — nay, anything at all like them; for the necessary insulation of race, of country, of religion, is impossible, even were it desirable. Journalism, translation, criticism, and facility of intercourse tend continually more and more to make the thought and turn of expression in cultivated men identical all over the world. Whether we like it or not, the costume of mind and body is gradually becoming of one cut.

W. D. HOWELLS
VENETIAN LIFE

THOSE of our readers who watch with any interest
the favorable omens of our literature from time to
time, must have had their eyes drawn to short poems,
remarkable for subtilty of sentiment and delicacy of
expression, and bearing the hitherto unfamiliar name
of Mr. Howells. Such verses are not common anywhere; as the work of a young man they are very uncommon. Youthful poets commonly begin by trying
on various manners before they settle upon any single one that is prominently their own. But what especially interested us in Mr. Howells was, that his
writings were from the very first not merely tentative
and preliminary, but had somewhat of the conscious
security of matured *style*. This is something which
most poets arrive at through much tribulation. It is
something which has nothing to do with the measure
of their intellectual powers or of their moral insight,
but is the one quality which essentially distinguishes
the artist from the mere man of genius. Among the
English poets of the last generation, Keats is the only
one who early showed unmistakable signs of it, and
developed it more and more fully until his untimely
death. Wordsworth, though in most respects a far
profounder man, attained it only now and then,

[146   ]

indeed only once perfectly, — in his "Laodamia."
Now, though it be undoubtedly true from one point
of view that what a man has to say is of more importance than how he says it, and that modern criticism
especially is more apt to be guided by its moral and
even political sympathies than by æsthetic princi-
ples, it remains as true as ever that only those things
have been said finally which have been said perfectly, and that this finished utterance is peculiarly
the office of poetry, or of what, for want of some word
as comprehensive as the German *Dichtung*, we are
forced to call imaginative literature. Indeed, it may
be said that, in whatever kind of writing, it is style
alone that is able to hold the attention of the world
long. Let a man be never so rich in thought, if he is
clumsy in the expression of it, his sinking, like that of
an old Spanish treasureship, will be hastened by the
very weight of his bullion, and perhaps, after the
lapse of a century, some lucky diver fishes up his
ingots and makes a fortune out of him.

That Mr. Howells gave unequivocal indications of
possessing this fine quality interested us in his modest
preludings. Marked, as they no doubt were, by some
uncertainty of aim and indefiniteness of thought,
that "stinting," as Chaucer calls it, of the nightin-
gale "ere he beginneth sing," there was nothing in
them of the presumption and extravagance which
young authors are so apt to mistake for originality

and vigor. Sentiment predominated over reflection, as was fitting in youth; but there was a refinement, an instinctive reserve of phrase, and a felicity of epithet, only too rare in modern, and especially in American writing. He was evidently a man more eager to make something good than to make a sensation, — one of those authors more rare than ever in our day of hand-to-mouth cleverness, who has a conscious ideal of excellence, and, as we hope, the patience that will at length reach it. We made occasion to find out something about him, and what we learned served to increase our interest. This delicacy, it appeared, was a product of the rough-and-ready West, this finish the natural gift of a young man with no advantage of college-training, who, passing from the compositor's desk to the editorship of a local newspaper, had been his own faculty of the humanities. But there are some men who are born cultivated. A singular fruit, we thought, of our shaggy democracy, — as interesting a phenomenon in that regard as it has been our fortune to encounter. Where is the rudeness of a new community, the pushing vulgarity of an imperfect civilization, the licentious contempt of forms that marks our unchartered freedom, and all the other terrible things which have so long been the bugaboos of European refinement? Here was a natural product, as perfectly natural as the deliberate attempt of "Walt Whitman" to answer the demand of native

[148]

and foreign misconception was perfectly artificial. Our institutions do not, then, irretrievably doom us to coarseness and to impatience of that restraining precedent which alone makes true culture possible and true art attainable. Unless we are mistaken, there is something in such an example as that of Mr. Howells which is a better argument for the American social and political system than any empirical theories that can be constructed against it.

We know of no single word which will so fitly characterize Mr. Howells's new volume about Venice as "delightful." The artist has studied his subject for four years, and at last presents us with a series of pictures having all the charm of tone and the minute fidelity to nature which were the praise of the Dutch school of painters, but with a higher sentiment, a more refined humor, and an airy elegance that recalls the better moods of Watteau. We do not remember any Italian studies so faithful or the result of such continuous opportunity, unless it be the "Roba di Roma" of Mr. Story, and what may be found scattered in the works of Henri Beyle. But Mr. Story's volumes recorded only the chance observations of a quick and familiar eye in the intervals of a profession to which one must be busily devoted who would rise to the acknowledged eminence occupied by their author; and Beyle's mind, though singularly acute and penetrating, had too much of the hardness of a man of the world and of Parisian cynicism to be altogether agreeable. Mr. Howells, during four years of that consular leisure which only Venice could make tolerable, devoted himself to the minute study of the superb prison to which he was doomed, and his book is his "Prigioni." Venice has been the university in which he has fairly earned the degree of Master. There is, perhaps, no European city, not even Bruges, not even Rome herself, which, not yet in ruins, is so wholly of the past, at once alive and turned to marble, like the Prince of the Black Islands in the story. And what gives it a peculiar fascination is that its antiquity, though venerable, is yet modern, and, so to speak, continuous; while that of Rome belongs half to a former world and half to this, and is broken irretrievably in two. The glory of Venice, too, was the achievement of her own genius, not an inheritance; and, great no longer, she is more truly than any other city the monument of her own greatness. She is something wholly apart, and the silence of her watery streets accords perfectly with the spiritual mood which makes us feel as if we were passing through a city of dream. Fancy now an imaginative young man from Ohio, where the log-hut was but yesterday turned to almost less enduring brick and mortar, set down suddenly in the midst of all this almost immemorial permanence of grandeur. We cannot think of any one on whom the impression would be so strangely deep, or whose eyes would be so quickened by the constantly recurring shock of unfamiliar objects. Most men are poor observers, because they are cheated into a delusion of intimacy with the things so long and so immediately about them; but surely we may hope for something like seeing from fresh eyes, and those too a poet's, when they open suddenly on a marvel so utterly alien to their daily vision and so perdurably novel as Venice. Nor does Mr. Howells disappoint our expectation. We have here something like a full-length portrait of the Lady of the Lagoons.

We have been struck in this volume, as elsewhere in writings of the same author, with the charm of *tone* that pervades it. It is so constant as to bear witness, not only to a real gift, but to the thoughtful cultivation of it. Here and there Mr. Howells yields to the temptation of *execution*, to which persons specially felicitous in language are liable, and pushes his experiments of expression to the verge of being unidiomatic, in his desire to squeeze the last drop of significance from words; but this is seldom, and generally we receive that unconscious pleasure in reading him which comes of naturalness, the last and highest triumph of good writing. Mr. Howells, of all men, does not need to be told that, as wine of the highest flavor and most delicate *bouquet* is made from juice pressed out by the unaided weight of the grapes, so in expression we are in danger of getting something like acridness if we crush in with the first sprightly runnings the skins and kernels of words in our vain hope to win more than we ought of their color and meaning. But, as we have said, this is rather a temptation to which he now and then shows himself liable, than a fault for which he can often be blamed. If a mind open to all poetic impressions, a sensibility too sincere ever to fall into maudlin sentimentality, a style flexible and sweet without weakness, and a humor which, like the bed of a stream, is the support of deep feeling, and shows waveringly through it in spots of full sunshine, — if such qualities can make a truly delightful book, then Mr. Howells has made one in the volume before us. And we give him warning that much will be expected of one who at his years has already shown himself capable of so much.

EDGAR A. POE [1]

THE situation of American literature is anomalous. It has no centre, or, if it have, it is like that of the sphere of Hermes. It is divided into many systems, each revolving round its several sun, and often presenting to the rest only the faint glimmer of a milk-and-water way. Our capital city, unlike London or Paris, is not a great central heart, from which life and vigor radiate to the extremities, but resembles more an isolated umbilicus, stuck down as near as may be to the centre of the land, and seeming rather to tell a legend of former usefulness than to serve any present need. Boston, New York, Philadelphia, each has its literature almost more distinct than those of the different dialects of Germany; and the Young Queen of the West has also one of her own, of which some articulate rumor barely has reached us dwellers by the Atlantic.

Perhaps there is no task more difficult than the just criticism of cotemporary literature. It is even more grateful to give praise where it is needed than

---

[1] The following notice of Mr. Poe's life and works was written at his own request, and accompanied a portrait of him published in *Graham's Magazine* for February, 1845. It is here [in R. W. Griswold's edition of Poe's Works (1850)] given with a few alterations and omissions.

where it is deserved, and friendship so often seduces the iron stylus of justice into a vague flourish, that she writes what seems rather like an epitaph than a criticism. Yet if praise be given as an alms, we could not drop so poisonous a one into any man's hat. The critic's ink may suffer equally from too large an infusion of nutgalls or of sugar. But it is easier to be generous than to be just, and we might readily put faith in that fabulous direction to the hiding-place of truth, did we judge from the amount of water which we usually find mixed with it.

Remarkable experiences are usually confined to the inner life of imaginative men, but Mr. Poe's biography displays a vicissitude and peculiarity of interest such as is rarely met with. The offspring of a romantic marriage, and left an orphan at an early age, he was adopted by Mr. Allan, a wealthy Virginian, whose barren marriage-bed seemed the warranty of a large estate to the young poet. Having received a classical education in England, he returned home and entered the University of Virginia, where, after an extravagant course, followed by reformation at the last extremity, he was graduated with the highest honors of his class. Then came a boyish attempt to join the fortunes of the insurgent Greeks, which ended at St. Petersburg, where he got into difficulties through want of a passport, from which he was rescued by the American consul, and sent home.[1] He now entered the military academy at West Point from which he obtained a dismissal on hearing of the birth of a son to his adopted father, by a second marriage, an event which cut off his expectations as an heir. The death of Mr. Allan, in whose will his name was not mentioned, soon after relieved him of all doubt in this regard, and he committed himself at once to authorship for a support. Previously to this, however, he had published (in 1827) a small volume of poems, which soon ran through three editions, and excited high expectations of its author's future distinction in the minds of many competent judges.

That no certain augury can be drawn from a poet's earliest lispings there are instances enough to prove. Shakespeare's first poems, though brimful of vigor and youth and picturesqueness, give but a very faint promise of the directness, condensation, and overflowing moral of his maturer works. Perhaps, however, Shakespeare is hardly a case in point, his "Venus and Adonis" having been published, we believe, in his twenty-sixth year. Milton's Latin verses show tenderness, a fine eye for nature, and a delicate appreciation of classic models, but give no hint of the author of a new style in poetry. Pope's youthful pieces have all the sing-song, wholly unrelieved by

[1] There is little evidence for this story, which some biographers have dismissed as a myth created by Poe himself. See Woodberry's *Poe*, v. i, p. 337.

the glittering malignity and eloquent irreligion of his later productions. Collins' callow namby-pamby died and gave no sign of the vigorous and original genius which he afterwards displayed. We have never thought that the world lost more in the "marvellous boy," Chatterton, than a very ingenious imitator of obscure and antiquated dulness. Where he becomes original (as it is called) the interest of ingenuity ceases and he becomes stupid. Kirke White's promises were endorsed by the respectable name of Mr. Southey but surely with no authority from Apollo. They have the merit of a traditional piety, which, to our mind, if uttered at all, had been less objectionable in the retired closet of a diary, and in the sober raiment of prose. They do not clutch hold of the memory with the drowning pertinacity of Watts; neither have they the interest of his occasional simple, lucky beauty. Burns, having fortunately been rescued by his humble station from the contaminating society of the "best models" wrote well and naturally from the first. Had he been unfortunate enough to have had an educated taste, we should have had a series of poems from which, as from his letters, we could sift here and there a kernel from the mass of chaff. Coleridge's youthful efforts give no promise whatever of that poetical genius which produced at once the wildest, tenderest, most original and most purely imaginative poems of modern times. Byron's

"Hours of Idleness" would never find a reader except from an intrepid and indefatigable curiosity. In Wordsworth's first preludings there is but a dim foreboding of the creator of an era. From Southey's early poems, a safer augury might have been drawn. They show the patient investigator, the close student of history, and the unwearied explorer of the beauties of predecessors, but they give no assurances of a man who should add aught to stock of household words, or to the rarer and more sacred delights of the fireside or the arbor. The earliest specimens of Shelley's poetic mind already, also, give tokens of that ethereal sublimation in which the spirit seems to soar above the regions of words, but leaves its body, the verse, to be entombed, without hope of resurrection, in a mass of them. Cowley is generally instanced as a wonder of precocity. But his early insipidities show only a capacity for rhyming and for the metrical arrangement of certain conventional combinations of words, a capacity wholly dependent on a delicate physical organization, and an unhappy memory. An early poem is only remarkable when it displays an effort of *reason*, and the rudest verses in which we can trace some conception of the ends of poetry, are worth all the miracles of smooth juvenile versification. A schoolboy, one would say, might acquire the regular see-saw of Pope merely by an association with the motion of the play-ground tilt.

Mr. Poe's early productions show that he could see through the verse to the spirit beneath, and that he already had a feeling that all the life and grace of the one must depend on and be modulated by the will of the other. We call them the most remarkable boyish poems that we have ever read. We know of none that can compare with them for maturity of purpose, and a nice understanding of the effects of language and metre. Such pieces are only valuable when they display what we can only express by the contradictory phrase of *innate experience*. We copy one of the shorter poems, written when the author was only fourteen. There is a little dimness in the filling up, but the grace and symmetry of the outline are such as few poets ever attain. There is a smack of ambrosia about it.

TO HELEN

Helen, thy beauty is to me
  Like those Nicean barks of yore,
That gently, o'er a perfumed sea,
  The weary, way-worn wanderer bore
  To his own native shore.

On desperate seas long wont to roam,
  Thy hyacinth hair, thy classic face,
Thy Naiad airs have brought me home
  To the glory that was Greece
  And the grandeur that was Rome.

Lo! in yon brilliant window-niche
  How statue-like I see thee stand!
The agate lamp within thy hand,
  Ah! Psyche, from the regions which
  Are Holy Land!

EDGAR A. POE

It is the *tendency* of the young poet that impresses us. Here is no "withering scorn," no heart "blighted" ere it has safely got into its teens, none of the drawing-room sans-culottism which Byron had brought into vogue. All is limpid and serene, with a pleasant dash of the Greek Helicon in it. The melody of the whole, too, is remarkable. It is not of that kind which can be demonstrated arithmetically upon the tips of the fingers. It is of that finer sort which the inner ear alone can estimate. It seems simple, like a Greek column, because of its perfection. In a poem named "Ligeia," under which title he intended to personify the music of nature, our boy-poet gives us the following exquisite picture:

> Ligeia! Ligeia!
>   My beautiful one,
> Whose harshest idea
>   Will to melody run,
> *Say, is it thy will,*
>   *On the breezes to toss,*
> *Or, capriciously still,*
>   *Like the lone albatross,*
> *Incumbent on night,*
>   *As she on the air,*
> *To keep watch with delight*
>   *On the harmony there?*

John Neal, himself a man of genius, and whose lyre has been too long capriciously silent, appreciated the high merit of these and similar passages, and drew a proud horoscope for their author.

Mr. Poe had that indescribable something which men have agreed to call *genius*. No man could ever tell us precisely what it is, and yet there is none who is not inevitably aware of its presence and its power. Let talent writhe and contort itself as it may, it has no such magnetism. Larger of bone and sinew it may be, but the wings are wanting. Talent sticks fast to earth, and its most perfect works have still one foot of clay. Genius claims kindred with the very workings of Nature herself, so that a sunset shall seem like a quotation from Dante or Milton, and if Shakespeare be read in the very presence of the sea itself, his verses shall but seem nobler for the sublime criticism of ocean. Talent may make friends for itself, but only genius can give to its creations the divine power of winning love and veneration. Enthusiasm cannot cling to what itself is unenthusiastic, nor will he ever have disciples who has not himself impulsive zeal enough to be a disciple. Great wits are allied to madness only inasmuch as they are possessed and carried away by their demon, while talent keeps him, as Paracelsus did, securely prisoned in the pommel of its sword. To the eye of genius, the veil of the spiritual world is ever rent asunder, that it may perceive the ministers of good and evil who throng continually around it. No man of mere talent ever flung his inkstand at the devil.

When we say that Mr. Poe had genius, we do not

mean to say that he has produced evidence of the highest. But to say that he possesses it at all is to say that he needs only zeal, industry, and a reverence for the trust reposed in him, to achieve the proudest triumphs and the greenest laurels. If we may believe the Longinuses and Aristotles of our newspapers, we have quite too many geniuses of the loftiest order to render a place among them at all desirable, whether for its hardness of attainment or its seclusion. The highest peak of our Parnassus is, according to these gentlemen, by far the most thickly settled portion of the country, a circumstance which must make it an uncomfortable residence for individuals of a poetical temperament, if love of solitude be, as immemorial tradition asserts, a necessary part of their idiosyncrasy.

Mr. Poe has two of the prime qualities of genius, a faculty of vigorous yet minute analysis, and a wonderful fecundity of imagination. The first of these faculties is as needful to the artist in words, as a knowledge of anatomy is to the artist in colors or in stone. This enables him to conceive truly, to maintain a proper relation of parts, and to draw a correct outline, while the second groups, fills up, and colors. Both of these Mr. Poe has displayed with singular distinctness in his prose works, the last predominating in his earlier tales, and the first in his later ones. In judging of the merit of an author, and assigning him his niche among our household gods, we have a right to regard him from our own point of view, and to measure him by our own standard. But, in estimating the amount of power displayed in his works, we must be governed by his own design, and, placing them by the side of his own ideal, find how much is wanting. We differ from Mr. Poe in his opinions of the objects of art. He esteems that object to be the creation of Beauty, and perhaps it is only in the definition of that word that we disagree with him. But in what we shall say of his writings, we shall take his own standard as our guide. The temple of the god of song is equally accessible from every side, and there is room enough in it for all who bring offerings, or seek an oracle.

In his tales, Mr. Poe has chosen to exhibit his power chiefly in that dim region which stretches from the very utmost limits of the probable into the weird confines of superstition and unreality. He combines in a very remarkable manner two faculties which are seldom found united; a power of influencing the mind of the reader by the impalpable shadows of mystery, and a minuteness of detail which does not leave a pin or a button unnoticed. Both are, in truth, the natural results of the predominating quality of his mind, to which we have before alluded, analysis. It is this which distinguishes the artist. His mind at once reaches forward to the

[162]

effect to be produced. Having resolved to bring about certain emotions in the reader, he makes all subordinate parts tend strictly to the common centre. Even his mystery is mathematical to his own mind. To him x is a known quantity all along. In any picture that he paints, he understands the chemical properties of all his colors. However vague some of his figures may seem, however formless the shadows, to him the outline is as clear and distinct as that of a geometrical diagram. For this reason Mr. Poe has no sympathy with *Mysticism*. The Mystic dwells *in* the mystery, is enveloped with it; it colors all his thoughts; it affects his optic nerve especially, and the commonest things get a rainbow edging from it. Mr. Poe, on the other hand, is a spectator *ab extrà*. He analyzes, he dissects, he watches

—— with an eye serene,
The very pulse of the machine,

for such it practically is to him, with wheels and cogs and piston-rods, all working to produce a certain end.

This analyzing tendency of his mind balances the poetical, and, by giving him the patience to be minute, enables him to throw a wonderful reality into his most unreal fancies. A monomania he paints with great power. He loves to dissect one of these cancers of the mind, and to trace all the subtle ramifications of its roots. In raising images of horror,

also, he has a strange success; conveying to us sometimes by a dusky hint some terrible *doubt* which is
the secret of all horror. He leaves to imagination the
task of finishing the picture, a task to which only she
is competent.

> For much imaginary work was there;
> Conceit deceitful, so compact, so kind,
> That for Achilles' image stood his spear
> Grasped in an armed hand; himself behind
> Was left unseen, save to the eye of mind.

Beside the merit of conception, Mr. Poe's writings
have also that of form. His style is highly finished,
graceful and truly classical. It would be hard to find
a living author who had displayed such varied powers. As an example of his style we would refer to one
of his tales, "The House of Usher," in the first volume
of his "Tales of the Grotesque and Arabesque." It
has a singular charm for us, and we think that no one
could read it without being strongly moved by its
serene and sombre beauty. Had its author written
nothing else, it would alone have been enough to
stamp him as a man of genius, and the master of a
classic style. In this tale occurs, perhaps, the most
beautiful of his poems.

The great masters of imagination have seldom
resorted to the vague and the unreal as sources of
effect. They have not used dread and horror alone,
but only in combination with other qualities, as
means of subjugating the fancies of their readers.

EDGAR A. POE

The loftiest muse has ever a household and fireside charm about her. Mr. Poe's secret lies mainly in the skill with which he has employed the strange fascination of mystery and terror. In this his success is so great and striking as to deserve the name of art, not artifice. We cannot call his materials the noblest or purest, but we must concede to him the highest merit of construction.

As a critic, Mr. Poe was æsthetically deficient. Unerring in his analysis of dictions, metres, and plots, he seemed wanting in the faculty of perceiving the profounder ethics of art. His criticisms are, however, distinguished for scientific precision and coherence of logic. They have the exactness, and at the same time, the coldness of mathematical demonstrations. Yet they stand in strikingly refreshing contrast with the vague generalisms and sharp personalities of the day. If deficient in warmth, they are also without the heat of partizanship. They are especially valuable as illustrating the great truth, too generally overlooked, that analytic power is a subordinate quality of the critic.

On the whole, it may be considered certain that Mr. Poe has attained an individual eminence in our literature, which he will keep. He has given proof of power and originality. He has done that which could only be done once with success or safety, and the imitation or repetition of which would produce weariness.

THACKERAY

ROUNDABOUT PAPERS

THE shock which was felt in this country at the sudden death of Thackeray was a new proof, if any were wanting, that London is still our social and literary capital. Not even the loss of Irving called forth so universal and strong an expression of sorrow. And yet it had been the fashion to call Thackeray a cynic. We must take leave to doubt whether Diogenes himself, much less any of his disciples, would have been so tenderly regretted. We think there was something more in all this than mere sentiment at the startling extinction of a great genius. There was a universal feeling that we had lost something even rarer and better, — a true man.

Thackeray was not a cynic, for the simple reason that he was a humorist, and could not have been one if he would. Your true cynic is a sceptic also; he is distrustful by nature, his laugh is a bark of selfish suspicion, and he scorns man, not because he has fallen below himself, but because he can rise no higher. But humor of the truest quality always rests on a foundation of belief in something better than it sees, and its laugh is a sad one at the awkward contrast between man as he is and man as he might be, between the real snob and the ideal image of his

Creator. Swift is our true English cynic, with his corrosive sarcasm; the satire of Thackeray is the recoil of an exquisite sensibility from the harsh touch of life. With all his seeming levity, Thackeray used to say, with the warmest sincerity, that Carlyle was his master and teacher. He had not merely a smiling contempt, but a deadly hatred, of all manner of *shams*, an equally intense love for every kind of manliness, and for gentlemanliness as its highest type. He had an eye for pretension as fatally detective as an acid for an alkali; wherever it fell, so clear and seemingly harmless, the weak spot was sure to betray itself. He called himself a disciple of Carlyle, but would have been the first to laugh at the absurdity of making any comparison between the playful heat-lightnings of his own satire and that lurid light, as of the Divine wrath over the burning cities of the plain, that flares out on us from the profoundest humor of modern times. Beside that *ingenium perfervidum* of the Scottish seer, he was but a Pall-Mall Jeremiah after all.

It is curious to see how often Nature, original and profuse as she is, repeats herself; how often, instead of sending one complete mind like Shakespeare, she sends two who are the complements of each other, — Fielding and Richardson, Goethe and Schiller, Balzac and George Sand, and now again Thackeray and Dickens. We are not fond of comparative criticism, we mean of that kind which brings forward the merit of one man as if it depreciated the different merit of another, nor of supercilious criticism, which measures every talent by some ideal standard of possible excellence, and, if it fall short, can find nothing to admire. A thing is either good in itself or good for nothing. Yet there is such a thing as a contrast of differences between two eminent intellects by which we may perhaps arrive at a clearer perception of what is characteristic in each. It is almost impossible, indeed, to avoid some sort of parallel *à la* Plutarch between Thackeray and Dickens. We do not intend to make out which is the greater, for they may be equally great, though utterly unlike, but merely to touch on a few striking points. Thackeray, in his more elaborate works, always paints character, and Dickens single peculiarities. Thackeray's personages are all men, those of Dickens personified oddities. The one is an artist, the other a caricaturist; the one pathetic, the other sentimental. Nothing is more instructive than the difference between the illustrations of their respective works. Thackeray's figures are such as we meet about the streets, while the artists who draw for Dickens invariably fall into the exceptionally grotesque. Thackeray's style is perfect, that of Dickens often painfully mannered. Nor is the contrast less remarkable in the quality of character which each selects. Thackeray looks at life from the

[168]

club-house window, Dickens from the reporter's box in the police-court. Dickens is certainly one of the greatest comic writers that ever lived, and has perhaps created more types of oddity than any other. His faculty of observation is marvellous, his variety inexhaustible. Thackeray's round of character is very limited; he repeated himself continually, and, as we think, had pretty well emptied his stock of invention. But his characters are masterpieces, always governed by those average motives, and acted upon by those average sentiments, which all men have in common. They never act like heroes and heroines, but like men and women.

Thackeray's style is beyond praise, — so easy, so limpid, showing everywhere by unobtrusive allusions how rich he was in modern culture, it has the highest charm of gentlemanly conversation. And it was natural to him, — his early works ("The Great Hoggarty Diamond," for example) being as perfect, as low in tone, as the latest. He was in all respects the most finished example we have of what is called a man of the world. In the pardonable eulogies which were uttered in the fresh grief at his loss there was a tendency to set him too high. He was even ranked above Fielding, — a position which no one would have been so eager in disclaiming as himself. No, let us leave the old fames on their pedestals. Fielding is the greatest creative artist who has written in English since Shakespeare. Of a broader and deeper nature, of a larger brain than Thackeray, his theme is Man, as that of the latter is Society. The Englishman with whom Thackeray had most in common was Richard Steele, as these "Roundabout Papers" show plainly enough. He admired Fielding, but he loved Steele.

TWO GREAT AUTHORS

THE cathedral of St. Patrick's, dreary enough in itself, seems to grow damper and chillier as one's foot-
steps disturb the silence between the grave of its
famous Dean and that of Stella, in death as in life
near yet divided from him, as if to make their memories more inseparable and prolong the insoluble problem of their relation to each other. Nor was there
wanting, when we made our pilgrimage thither, a
touch of grim humor in the thought that our tipsy
guide (Clerk of the Works he had dubbed himself for
the nonce), as he monotonously recited his contradictory anecdotes of the "sullybrutted Dane," varied by
times with an irrelative hiccough of his own, was no
inapt type of the ordinary biographers of Swift. The
skill with which long practice had enabled our cice-
rone to turn these involuntary hitches of his discourse
into rhetorical flourishes, and well-nigh to make
them seem a new kind of conjunction, would have
been invaluable to the Dean's old servant Patrick,
but in that sad presence his grotesqueness was as
shocking as the clown in one of Shakespeare's trage-
dies to Châteaubriand. A shilling sent him back
to the neighboring pot-house whence a half-dozen

[1] [A review of *The Life of Jonathan Swift*, by John Forster.]

ragged volunteers had summoned him, and we were left to our musings. One dominating thought shouldered aside all others — namely, how strange a stroke of irony it was, how more subtle even than any of the master's own, that our most poignant association with the least sentimental of men should be one of sentiment, and that a romance second only to that of Abélard and Héloïse should invest the memory of him who had done more than all others together to strip life and human nature of their last instinctive decency of illusion. His life, or such accounts as we had of it, had been full of antitheses as startling as if some malign enchanter had embodied one of Macaulay's characters as a conundrum to bewilder the historian himself. A generous miser; a sceptical believer; a devout scoffer; a tender-hearted misanthrope; a churchman faithful to his order yet loathing to wear its uniform; an Irishman hating the Irish, as Heine did the Jews,[1] because he was one of them, yet defending them with the scornful fierceness

[1] Lowell was mistaken. Heine never lost his love for the Jews. He regretted his apostasy and always regarded himself as a Jew, and not a Christian. His own genius was Hebraic, and not, as Matthew Arnold thought, Hellenic. It should be incidentally stated that Lowell had great admiration for the Jews. The late Dr. Weir Mitchell once told me that Lowell regretted that he was not a Jew and even wished that he had a Hebraic nose. Several documents attest to Lowell's ideas on the subject. He even claimed that his middle name "Russell" showed that he had Jewish blood. A. M.

of one who hated their oppressors more; a man honest and of statesmanlike mind, who lent himself to the basest services of party politics for purely selfish ends; a poet whose predominant faculty was that of disidealizing; a master of vernacular style, in whose works an Irish editor finds hundreds of faults of English to correct; strangest of all, a middle-aged clergyman of brutal coarseness, who could inspire two young, beautiful, and clever women, the one with a fruitless passion that broke her heart, the other with a love that survived hope and faith to suck away the very sources of that life whereof it was the only pride and consolation. No wonder that a new life of so problematic a personage as this should be awaited with eagerness, the more that it was to be illustrated with much hitherto unpublished material and was to be written by the practised hand of Mr. Forster. Inconsistency of conduct, of professed opinion, whether of things or men, we can understand; but an inconsistent character is something without example, and which nature abhors as she does false logic. Opportunity may develop, hindrance may dwarf, the prevailing set of temptation may give a bent to character, but the germ planted at birth can never be wholly disnatured by circumstance any more than soil or exposure can change an oak into a pine. Character is continuous, it is cumulative, whether for good or ill; the general tenor of the life is a logical sequence from it, and a man can always explain himself to himself, if not to others, as a coherent whole, because he always knows, or thinks he knows, the value of x in the personal equation. Were it otherwise, that sense of conscious identity which alone makes life a serious thing and immortality a rational hope, would be impossible. It is with the means of finding out this unknown quantity — in other words, of penetrating to the man's motives or his understanding of them — that the biographer undertakes to supply us, and unless he succeed in this, his rummaging of old papers but raises a new cloud of dust to darken our insight.

If Mr. Forster's mind had not the penetrative, illuminating quality of genius, he was not without some very definite qualifications for his task. The sturdy temper of his intellect fits him for a subject which is beset with pitfalls for the sentimentalizer. A finer sense might recoil before investigations whose importance is not at first so clear as their promise of unsavoriness. So far as Mr. Forster has gone, we think he has succeeded in the highest duty of a biographer: that of making his subject interesting and humanly sympathetic to the reader — a feat surely of some difficulty with a professed cynic like Swift. He lets him in the main tell his own story — a method not always trustworthy, to be sure, but safer in the case of one who, whatever else he may have

been, was almost brutally sincere when he could be so
with safety or advantage. Still, it should always be
borne in mind that he *could* lie with an air of honest
candor fit to deceive the very elect. The author of
the "Battle of the Books" (written in 1697) tells us
in the preface to the Third Part of Temple's "Mis-
cellanea" (1701) that he "cannot well inform the
reader upon what occasion" the essay upon Ancient
and Modern Learning "was writ, having been at
that time in another kingdom"; and the professed
confidant of a ministry, whom the Stuart Papers
have proved to have been in correspondence with the
Pretender, puts on an air of innocence (in his "En-
quiry into the Behavior of the Queen's last Ministry") and undertakes to convince us that nothing
could be more absurd than to accuse them of Jacobit-
ism. It may be, as Orrery asserted, that Swift was
"employed, not trusted," but this is hardly to be
reconciled with Lewis's warning him on the Queen's
death to burn his papers, or his own jest to Harley
about the one being beheaded and the other hanged.
The fact is that, while in certain contingencies Swift
was as unscrupulous a liar as Voltaire, he was naturally open and truthful, and showed himself to be so
whenever his passions or his interest would let him.
That Mr. Forster should make a hero of the man
whose life he has undertaken to write is both natural
and proper; for without sympathy there can be no

right understanding, and a hearty admiration is alone capable of that generosity in the interpretation of conduct to which all men have a right, and which he needs most who most widely transcends the ordinary standards or most resolutely breaks with tradition- ary rules. That so virile a character as Swift should have been attractive to women is not wonderful, but we think Mr. Forster has gone far towards proving that he was capable of winning the deep and lasting affection of men also. Perhaps it may not always be safe to trust implicitly the fine phrases of his corre- spondents; for there can be no doubt that Swift in- spired fear as well as love. Revengefulness is the great and hateful blot on his character; his brooding tem- per turned slights into injuries, gave substance to mere suspicion, and once in the morbid mood he was utterly reckless of the means of vengeance. His most playful scratch had poison in it. His eye was equally terrible for the weak point of friend and foe. But giv- ing this all the value it may deserve, the weight of the evidence is in favor of his amiability. The testimony of a man so sweet-natured and fair-minded as Dr. Delany ought to be conclusive, and we do not won- der that Mr. Forster should lay great stress upon it. The depreciatory conclusions of Dr. Johnson are doubtless entitled to consideration; but his evidence is all from hearsay, and there were properties in Swift that aroused in him so hearty a moral repulsion as to disenable him for an unprejudiced opinion. Admirable as the rough-and-ready conclusions of his robust understanding often are, he was better fitted to reckon the quantity of a man's mind than the quality of it — the real test of its value; and there is something almost comically pathetic in the good faith with which he applies his beer-measure to juices that could fairly plead their privilege to be gauged by the wine standard. Mr. Forster's partiality qualifies him for a fairer judgment of Swift than any which Johnson was capable of forming, or, indeed, would have given himself the trouble to form.

But this partiality in a biographer, though to be allowed and even commended as a quickener of insight, should not be strong enough to warp his mind from its judicial level. While we think that Mr. Forster is mainly right in his estimate of Swift's character, and altogether so in insisting on trying him by documentary rather than hearsay evidence, it is equally true that he is sometimes betrayed into overestimates, and into positive statement, where favorable inference would have been wiser. Now and then his exaggeration is merely amusing, as where he tells us that Swift, "as early as in his first two years after quitting Dublin, was *accomplished in French*," the only authority for such a statement being a letter of recommendation from Temple saying that he "had *some French*." Such compulsory testimonials are not on their *voir dire* any more than epitaphs. So, in speaking of Betty Jones, with whom in 1689 Swift had a flirtation that alarmed his mother, Mr. Forster assumes that she "was an educated girl" on the sole ground, so far as appears, of "her mother and Swift's being cousins." Swift, to be sure, thirty years later, on receiving some letters from his old sweetheart, "suspects them to be counterfeit" because "she spells like a kitchen-maid," and this, perhaps, may be Mr. Forster's authority. But, as the letters *were* genuine, the inference should have been the other way. The "letters to Eliza," by the way, which Swift in 1699 directs Winder, his successor at Kilroot, to burn, were doubtless those addressed to Betty Jones. Mr. Forster does not notice this; but that Swift should have preserved them, or copies of them, is of some consequence, as tending to show that they were mere exercises in composition, thus confirming what he says in the remarkable letter to Kendall, written in 1692, when he was already off with the old love and on with a new.

These instances of the temptation which most easily besets Mr. Forster are trifles, but the same leaning betrays him sometimes into graver mistakes of overestimate. He calls Swift the best letter-writer in the language, though Gray, Walpole, Cowper, and Lamb be in some essential qualities his superiors. He praises his political writing so extravagantly that we

should think he had not read the "Examiner," were
it not for the thoroughness of his work in other respects. All that Swift wrote in this kind was partisan,
excellently fitted to its immediate purpose, as we
might expect from his imperturbable good sense, but
by its very nature ephemeral. There is none of that
reach of historical imagination, none of that grasp of
the clue of fatal continuity and progression, none of
that eye for country which divines the future high-
ways of events, that makes the occasional pam-
phlets of Burke, with all their sobs of passionate sentiment, permanent acquisitions of political thinking.
Mr. Forster finds in Swift's "Examiners" all the
characteristic qualities of his mind and style, though
we believe that a dispassionate reader would rather
conclude that the author, as we have little doubt was
the fact, was trying all along to conceal his personal-
ity under a disguise of decorous commonplace. In the
same uncritical way Mr. Forster tells us that "the
ancients could show no such humor and satire as the
'Tale of a Tub' and the 'Battle of the Books.'" In
spite of this, we shall continue to think Aristophanes
and even Lucian clever writers, considering the rudeness of the times in which they lived. The "Tale of a
Tub" has several passages of rough-and-tumble satire as good as any of their kind, and some hints of
deeper suggestion, but the fable is clumsy and the
execution unequal and disjointed. In conception the

"Battle" is cleverer, and it contains perhaps the most perfect apologue in the language, but the best strokes of satire in it are personal (that of Dryden's helmet, for instance), and we enjoy them with an uneasy feeling that we are accessaries in something like foul play. Indeed, it may be said of Swift's humor generally that it leaves us uncomfortable, and that it too often impregnates the memory with a savor of mortal corruption proof against all disinfectants. Pure humor cannot flow from so turbid a source as *sœva indignatio*, and if man be so filthy and disgusting a creature as Swift represents him to be, if he be truly "by nature, reason, learning, blind," satire is thrown away upon him for reform and cruel as castigation.

Mr. Forster not only rejects the story of Stella's marriage with Swift as lacking substantial evidence, but thinks that the limits of their intercourse were early fixed and never overpassed. According to him, their relation was to be, from the first, one "of affection, not desire." We, on the other hand, believe that she was the only woman Swift ever loved constantly, that he wished and meant to marry her, that he probably did marry her,[1] but only when all hope of the old open-hearted confidence was gone forever, chiefly through his own fault, if partly through her jealous misconception of his relation to Vanessa, and that it

[1] Most of the authorities conclude that Swift never married Stella. A. M.

was the sense of his own weakness, which admitted
of no explanation tolerable to an injured woman, and
entailed upon a brief folly all the consequences of
guilt, that more than all else darkened his lonely de-
cline with unavailing regrets and embittered it with
remorseful self-contempt. Nothing could be more
galling to a proud man than the feeling that he had
been betrayed by his vanity. It is commonly assumed that pride is incompatible with its weaker
congener. But pride, after all, is nothing more than a
stiffened and congealed vanity, and melts back to its
original ductility when exposed to the milder temperature of female partiality. Swift could not deny
himself the flattery of Vanessa's passion, and not to
forbid was to encourage. He could not bring himself
to administer in time the only effectual remedy, by
telling her that he was pledged to another woman.
When at last he did tell her it was too late; and he
learned, like so many before and since, that the most
dangerous of all fires to play with is that of love. This
was the extent of his crime, and it would have been
none if there had been no such previous impediment.
This alone gives any meaning to what he says when
Vanessa declared her love:

> Cadenus felt within him rise
> *Shame*, disappointment, *guilt*, surprise.

Shame there might have been, but surely no guilt on
any theory except that of an implicit engagement

with Stella. That there was something of the kind,
more or less definite, and that it was of some ten
years' standing when the affair with Vanessa came to
a crisis, we have no doubt. When Tisdall offered her
marriage in 1704, and Swift wrote to him "that if my
fortunes and humor served me to think of that state,
I should certainly, among all persons on earth, make
your choice," she accepted the implied terms and re-
jected her suitor, though otherwise not unacceptable
to her. She would wait. It is true that Swift had not
absolutely committed himself, but she had committed him by dismissing Tisdall. Without assuming
some such tacit understanding, his letters to her are
unintelligible. He repeatedly alludes to his absence
from her as only tolerable because it was for her sake
no less than his own, and the details of his petty
economies would be merely vulgar except to her for
whom their motive gave them a sweetness of humorous pathos. The evidence of the marriage seems to be
as conclusive as that of a secret can well be. Dr. Delany, who ought to have been able to judge of its
probability, and who had no conceivable motive of
misstatement, was assured of it by one whose authority was Stella herself. Mr. Monck-Berkeley had it
from the widow of Bishop Berkeley, and she from her
husband, who had it from Dr. Ashe, by whom they
were married. These are at least unimpeachable witnesses. The date of the marriage is more doubtful,

but Sheridan is probably not far wrong when he puts it in 1716. It was simply a reparation, and no union was implied in it. Delany intimates that Vanessa, like the young Chevalier, vulgarized her romance in drink. More than this, however, was needful to palliate even in Swift the brutal allusion to her importunacy in "Gulliver," unless, as is but too possible, the passage in question be an outbreak of ferocious spleen against her victorious rival. Its coarseness need not make this seem impossible, for that was by no means a queasy age, and Swift continued on intimate terms with Lady Betty Germaine after the publication of the nasty verses on her father. The communication of the secret to Bishop Berkeley (who was one of Vanessa's executors) may have been the condition of the suppressing Swift's correspondence with her, and would have exasperated him to ferocity.

II

WE cannot properly understand Swift's cynicism and bring it into any relation of consistency with our belief in his natural amiability without taking his whole life into account. Few give themselves the trouble to study his beginnings, and few, therefore, give weight enough to the fact that he made a false start. He, the ground of whose nature was an acrid common-sense, whose eye magnified the canker till it effaced the rose, began as what would now be called a romantic poet. With no mastery of verse, for even the English heroic (a balancing-pole which has enabled so many feebler men to walk the ticklish rope of momentary success) was uneasy to him, he essayed the Cowleian Pindarique, as the adjective was then rightly spelled with a hint of Parisian rather than Theban origin. If the master was but a fresh example of the disasters that wait upon every new trial of the flying-machine, what could be expected of the disciple who had not even the secret of the mechanic wings, and who stuck solidly to the earth while with perfect good faith he went through all the motions of soaring? Swift was soon aware of the ludicrousness of his experiment, though he never forgave Cousin Dryden for being aware of it also, and the recoil in a nature so intense as his was sudden and violent. He who could not be a poet if he would, angrily resolved that he would not if he could. Full-sail verse was beyond his skill, but he could manage the simpler fore-and-aft rig of Butler's octosyllabics. As Cowleyism was a trick of seeing everything as it was not, and calling everything something else than it was, he would see things as they were — or as, in his sullen disgust, they seemed to be — and call them all by their right names with a resentful emphasis. He achieved the naked sincerity of a Hottentot — nay, he even went beyond it in rejecting the feeble compromise of the breech-clout. Not

only would he be naked and not ashamed, but everybody else should be so with a blush of conscious exposure, and human nature should be stripped of the
hypocritical fig-leaves that betrayed by attempting
to hide its identity with the brutes that perish. His
sincerity was not unconscious, but self-willed and ag-
gressive. But it would be unjust to overlook that he
began with himself. He despised mankind because he
found something despicable in Jonathan Swift, as
he makes Gulliver hate the Yahoos in proportion to
their likeness with himself. He had more or less consciously sacrificed self-respect for that false consideration which is paid to a man's accidents; he had
preferred the vain pomp of being served on plate, as
no other "man of his level" in Ireland was, to being
happy with the woman who had sacrificed herself to
his selfishness, and the independence he had won
turned out to be only a morose solitude after all.
"Money," he was fond of saying, "is freedom," but
he never learned that self-denial is freedom with the
addition of self-respect. With a hearty contempt for
the ordinary objects of human ambition, he could
yet bring himself for the sake of them to be the
obsequious courtier of three royal strumpets. How
should he be happy who had defined happiness to be
"the perpetual possession of being well deceived,"
and who could never be deceived himself? It may
well be doubted whether what he himself calls "that

pretended philosophy which enters into the depth of things and then comes gravely back with informations and discoveries that in the inside they are good for nothing," be of so penetrative an insight as it is apt to suppose, and whether the truth be not rather that to the empty all things are empty. Swift's diseased eye had the microscopic quality of Gulliver's in Brobdingnag, and it was the loathsome obscenity which this revealed in the skin of things that tainted his imagination when it ventured on what was beneath. But with all Swift's scornful humor, he never made the pitiful mistake of his shallow friend Gay that life was a jest. To his nobler temper it was always profoundly tragic, and the salt of his sarcasm was more often, we suspect, than with most humorists distilled out of tears. The lesson is worth remembering that *his* apples of Sodom, like those of lesser men, were plucked from boughs of his own grafting.

But there are palliations for him, even if the world were not too ready to forgive a man everything if he will only be a genius. Sir Robert Walpole used to say "that it was fortunate so few men could be prime ministers, as it was best that few should thoroughly know the shocking wickedness of mankind." Swift, from his peculiar relation to two successive ministries, was in a position to know all that they knew, and perhaps, as a recognized place-broker, even more than they knew, of the selfish servility of men. He had seen the men who figure so imposingly in the stage-processions of history too nearly. He knew the real Jacks and Toms as they were over a pot of ale after the scenic illusion was done with. He saw the destinies of a kingdom controlled by men far less able than himself; the highest of arts, that of politics, degraded to a trade in places, and the noblest opportunity, that of office, abused for purposes of private gain. His disenchantment began early, probably in his intimacy with Sir William Temple, in whom (though he says that all that was good and great died with him) he must have seen the weak side of solemn priggery and the pretension that made a mystery of statecraft. In his twenty-second year he writes:

> Off fly the vizards and discover all:
>> How plain I see through the deceit!
>> How shallow and how gross the cheat!
>
> .   .   .   .
>> On what poor engines move
> The thoughts of monarchs and designs of states!
> What petty motives rule their fates!
>
>> I to such blockheads set my wit!
>> I damn such fools! go, go, you're bit!

Mr. Forster's own style (simpler now than when he was under the immediate influence of Dickens, if more slipshod than when repressed by Landor) is not in essentials better or worse than usual. It is not

always clear nor always idiomatic. On page 120 he
tells us that "Scott did not care to enquire if it was
likely that stories of the kind referred to should have
contributed to form a character, or if it were not
likelier still that they had grown and settled round a
character already famous as well as formed." Not to
speak of the confusion of moods and tenses, the
phrase "to form a character" has been so long ap-
propriated to another meaning than that which it
has here, that the sense of the passage vacillates un-
pleasantly. He tells us that Swift was "under engagement to Will Frankland to christen *the baby his wife
is near bringing to bed.*" Parthenogenesis is a simple
matter to this. And why *Will* Frankland, *Joe* Beau-
mont, and the like? We cannot claim so much intimacy with them as Swift, and the eighteenth century might be allowed to stand a little on its dignity.
If Mr. Forster had been quoting the journal to Stella,
there would be nothing to say except that Swift took
liberties with his friends in writing to her which he
would not have ventured on before strangers. In the
same odd jargon, which the English journals are
fond of calling American, Mr. Forster says that
"Tom [Leigh] was not *popular* with Swift." Mr.
Forster is not only no model for contemporary English, but (what is more serious) sometimes mistakes
the meaning of words in Swift's day, as when he
explains that "strongly engaged" meant "inter-

ceded with or pressed." It meant much more than
that, as could easily be shown from the writings of
Swift himself.

All the earlier biographers of Swift Mr. Forster
brushes contemptuously aside, though we do not
find much that is important in his own biography
which industry may not hit upon somewhere or
other in the confused narrative of Sheridan, for
whom and for his sources of information he shows a
somewhat unjust contempt. He goes so far as sometimes to discredit anecdotes so thoroughly characteristic of Swift that he cannot resist copying them
himself. He labors at needless length the question of
Swift's standing in college, and seems to prove that
it was not contemptible, though there can be no
doubt that the contrary opinion was founded on
Swift's own assertion, often repeated. We say he
seems to prove it, for we are by no means satisfied
which of the two Swifts on the college list, of which
a facsimile is given, is the future Dean. Mr. Forster
assumes that the names are ranked in the order of
seniority, but they are more likely to have been
arranged alphabetically, in which case Jonathan
would have preceded Thomas, and at best there is
little to choose between three *mediocriters* and one
male, one *bene*, and one *negligenter*. The document,
whatever we may think of its importance, has been
brought to light by Mr. Forster. Of his other mate-

rials hitherto unpublished, the most important is a letter proving that Swift's Whig friends did their best to make him a bishop in 1707. This shows that his own later account of the reasons of his change from Whig to Tory, if not absolutely untrue, is at least unjust to his former associates, and had been shaped to meet the charge of inconsistency if not of desertion to the enemy. Whatever the motives of his change, it would have been impossible to convince a sincere Whig of their honesty, and in spite of Mr. Forster's assertion that Addison continued to love and trust him to the last, we do not believe that there was any cordiality in their intercourse after 1710. No one familiar with Swift's manner of thinking will deem his political course of much import in judging of his moral character. At the bottom of his heart he had an impartial contempt for both parties, and a firm persuasion that the aims of both were more or less consciously selfish. Even if sincere, the matters at issue between them were as despicable to a sound judgment as that which divided the Big and Little-endians in Lilliput. With him the question was simply one between men who galled his pride and men who flattered it. Sunderland and Somers treated him as a serviceable inferior; Harley and Bolingbroke had the wit to receive him on a footing of friendship. To him they were all, more or less indifferently, rounds in the ladder by which he hoped to climb. He always claimed to have been a consistent Old Whig — that is, as he understood it, a High-Churchman who accepted the Revolution of 1688. This, to be sure, was not quite true, but it could not have been hard for a man who prided himself on a Cavalier grandfather, and whose first known verses were addressed to the non-juring primate Sancroft after his deprivation, to become first a Tory and then a conniver at the restoration of the Stuarts as the best device for preventing a foreign succession and an endless chance of civil war. A man of Swift's way of thinking would hardly have balked at the scruple of creed, for he would not have deemed it possible that the Pretender should have valued a kingdom at any lower rate than his great-grandfather had done before him.

The more important part of Mr. Forster's fresh material is to come in future volumes, if now, alas! we are ever to have them. For some of what he gives us in this we can hardly thank him. One of the manuscripts he has unearthed is the original version of "Baucis and Philemon" as it was before it had passed under the criticism of Addison. He seems to think it in some respects better than the revised copy, though in our judgment it entirely justifies the wisdom of the critic who counselled its curtailment and correction. The piece as we have hitherto had it comes as near poetry as anything Swift ever wrote except "Cadenus and Vanessa," though neither of them aspires above the region of cleverness and fancy. Indeed, it is misleading to talk of the poetry of one whose fatal gift was an eye that disidealized. But we are not concerned here with the discussion of Swift's claim to the title of poet. What we are concerned about is to protest in the interests of good literature against the practice, now too common, of hunting out and printing what the author would doubtless have burned. It is unfair to the dead writer and the living reader by disturbing that unitary impression which every good piece of work aims at making, and is sure to make, only in proportion to the author's self-denial and his skill in

The last and greatest art, the art to blot.

We do not wish, nor have we any right to know, those passages through which the castigating pen has been drawn.

Mr. Forster may almost claim to have rediscovered Swift's journals to Esther Johnson, to such good purpose has he used them in giving life and light to his narrative. He is certainly wrong, however, in saying to the disparagement of former editors that the name Stella was not invented "till long after all the letters were written." This statement, improbable in itself as respects a man who forthwith refined Betty, Waring, and Vanhomrigh into Eliza, Varina,

and Vanessa, is refuted by a passage in the journal of 14th October, 1710, printed by Mr. Forster
himself. At least, we know not what "Stellakins"
means unless it be "little Stella." The value of these
journals for their elucidation of Swift's character
cannot be overestimated, and Mr. Forster is quite
right in insisting upon the importance of the "little
language," though we are by no means sure that he
is always so in his interpretation of the cipher. It is
quite impossible, for instance, that ME can stand
for Madam Elderly, and so for Dingley. It is certainly addressed, like the other endearing epithets,
to Esther Johnson, and may mean My Esther or
even Marry Esther, for anything we know to the
contrary.

Mr. Forster brings down his biography no farther
than the early part of 1710, so that we have no means
of judging what his opinion would be of the conduct
of Swift during the three years that preceded the
death of Queen Anne. But he has told us what he
thinks of his relations with Esther Johnson; and it
is in them, as it seems to us, that we are to seek the
key to the greater part of what looks most enig-
matical in his conduct. At first sight, it seems altogether unworthy of a man of Swift's genius to waste
so much of it and so many of the best years of his
life in a sordid struggle after preferment in the church
— a career in which such selfish ambitions look most

out of place. How much better to have stayed quietly at Laracor and written immortal works! Very good: only that was not Swift's way of looking at the matter, who had little appetite for literary fame, and all of whose immortal progeny were begotten of the moment's overmastering impulse, were thrown nameless upon the world by their father, and survived only in virtue of the vigor they had drawn from his stalwart loins. But how if Swift's worldly aspirations, and the intrigues they involved him in, were not altogether selfish? How if he was seeking advancement, in part at least, for another, and that other a woman who had sacrificed for him not only her chances of domestic happiness, but her good name? to whom he was bound by gratitude? and the hope of repairing whose good fame by making her his own was so passionate in that intense nature as to justify any and every expedient, and make the patronage of those whom he felt to be his inferiors endurable by the proudest of men? We believe that this was the truth, and that the woman was Stella. No doubt there were other motives. Coming to manhood with a haughtiness of temper that was almost savage, he had forced himself to endure the hourly humiliation of what could not have been, however Mr. Forster may argue to the contrary, much above domestic servitude. This experience deepened in him the prevailing passions of his life, first for independence and next for consideration, the only ones which could, and in the end perhaps did, obscure the memory and hope of Stella. That he should have longed for London with a persistency that submitted to many a rebuff and overlived continual disappointment will seem childish only to those who do not consider that it was a longing for life. It was there only that his mind could be quickened by the society and spur of equals. In Dublin he felt it dying daily of the inanition of inferior company. His was not a nature, if there be any such, that could endure the solitude of supremacy without impair, and he foreboded with reason a Tiberian old age.

This certainly is not the ordinary temper of a youth on whom the world is just opening. In a letter to Pope, written in 1725, he says, "I desire that you and all my friends will take a special care that my disaffection to the world may not be imputed to my age; for I have credible witnesses ready to depose that it hath never varied from the twenty-first to the fifty-eighth year of my age." His contempt for mankind would not be lessened by his knowledge of the lying subterfuges by which the greatest poet of his age sought at once to gratify and conceal his own vanity, nor by listening to the professions of its cleverest statesman that he liked planting cabbages better than being prime minister. How he must have laughed at the unconscious parody when his old printer Barber wrote to him in the same strain of philosophic relief from the burthensome glories of lord-mayoralty!

Nay, he made another false start, and an irreparable one, in prose also with the "Tale of a Tub." Its levity, if it was not something worse, twice balked him of the mitre when it seemed just within his reach. Justly or not, he had the reputation of scepticism. Mr. Forster would have us believe him devout, but the evidence goes no further than to prove him ceremonially decorous. Certain it is that his most intimate friends, except Arbuthnot, were free-thinkers, and wrote to him sometimes in a tone that was at least odd in addressing a clergyman. Probably the feeling that he had made a mistake in choosing a profession which was incompatible with success in politics, and with perfect independence of mind, soured him even more than his disappointed hopes. He saw Addison a secretary of state and Prior an ambassador, while he was bubbled (as he would have put it) with a shabby deanery among savages. Perhaps it was not altogether his clerical character that stood in his way. A man's little faults are more often the cause of his greatest miscarriages than he is able to conceive, and in whatever respects his two friends might have been his inferiors, they certainly had the advantage of him in that *savoir vivre* which makes so large an element of worldly success. In judging him, however, we must take into account that his first literary hit was made when he was already thirty-seven, with a confirmed bias towards moody suspicion of others and distrust of himself.

The reaction in Swift's temper and ambition told with the happiest effect on his prose. For its own purposes, as good working English, his style (if that may be called so whose chief success was that it had no style at all), has never been matched. It has been more praised than studied, or its manifest short-comings, its occasional clumsiness, its want of har-mony and of feeling for the finer genialities of language, would be more often present in the con-sciousness of those who discourse about it from a superficial acquaintance. With him language was a means and not an end. If he was plain and even coarse, it was from choice rather than because he lacked delicacy of perception; for in badinage, the most ticklish use to which words can be put, he was a master.

PLUTARCH'S MORALS [1]

PLUTARCH is perhaps the most eminent example of how strong a hold simple good humor and good sense lay upon the affections of mankind. Not a man of genius or heroism himself, his many points of sympathy with both make him an admirable conductor of them in that less condensed form which is more wholesome and acceptable to the average mind. Of no man can it be more truly said that, if not a rose himself, he had lived all his days in the rose's neighborhood. Such is the delightful equableness of his temperament and his singular talent for reminiscence, so far is he always from undue heat while still susceptible of so much enthusiasm as shall not disturb digestion, that he might seem to have been born middle-aged. Few men have so amicably combined the love of a good dinner and of the higher morality. He seems to have comfortably solved the problem of having your cake and eating it, at which the ascetic interpreters of Christianity teach us to despair. He serves us up his worldly wisdom in a sauce of Plato, and gives a kind of sensuous relish to the disembodied satisfactions of immortality. He is a better Christian than many an orthodox divine. If he

[1] [A review of the English translation edited by William W. Goodwin with an Introduction by Ralph Waldo Emerson.]

[200]

do not, like Sir Thomas Browne, love to lose himself in an *O, altitudo!* yet the sky-piercing peaks and snowy solitudes of ethical speculation loom always on the horizon about the sheltered dwelling of his mind, and he continually gets up from his books to rest and refresh his eyes upon them. He seldom invites us to alpine-climbing, and when he does, it is to some warm nook like the Jardin on Mont Blanc, a parenthesis of homely summer nestled amid the sublime nakedness of snow. If he glance upward at becoming intervals to the "primal duties," he turns back with a settled predilection to the "sympathies that are nestled at the feet like flowers." But it is within his villa that we love to be admitted to him and to enjoy that garrulity which we forgive more readily in the mother of the muses than in any of her daughters, unless it be Clio, who is most like her. If we are in the library, he is reminded of this or that passage in a favorite author, and, going to the shelves, takes down the volume to read it aloud with decorous emphasis. If we are in the *atrium* (where we like him best) he has an anecdote to tell of all the great Greeks and Romans whose busts or statues are ranged about us, and who for the first time soften from their marble alienation and become human. It is this that makes him so amiable a moralist and brings his lessons home to us. He does not preach up any remote and inaccessible virtue, but makes all his lessons of magnanimity, self-devotion, patriotism, seem neighborly and practicable to us by an example which associates them with our common humanity. His higher teaching is theosophy with no taint of theology. He is a pagan Tillotson disencumbered of the archiepiscopal robes, a practical Christian unbewildered with doctrinal punctilios. This is evidently what commended him as a philosopher to Montaigne, as may be inferred from some hints which follow immediately upon the comparison between Seneca and Plutarch in the essay on "Physiognomy." After speaking of some "escripts encores plus révérez," he asks, in his idiomatic way, "à quoy faire nous allons nous gendarmant par ces efforts de la science?" More than this, however, Montaigne liked him because he was *good talk*, as it is called, a better companion than writer. Yet he is not without passages which are noble in point of mere style. Landor remarks this in the conversation between Johnson and Tooke, where he makes Tooke say: "Although his style is not valued by the critics, I could inform them that there are in Plutarch many passages of exquisite beauty, in regard to style, derived perhaps from authors much more ancient." But if they are borrowed, they have none of the discordant effect of the *purpureus pannus*, for the warm sympathy of his nature assimilates them thoroughly and makes them his own. Oddly enough, it is through his memory that

[202]

Plutarch is truly original. Who ever remembered so
much and yet so well? It is this selectness (without
being overfastidious) that gauges the natural eleva-
tion of his mind. He is a gossip, but he has supped
with Plato or sat with Alexander in his tent to bring
away only memorable things. We are speaking of
him, of course, at his best. Many of his essays are
trivial, but there is hardly one whose sands do not
glitter here and there with the proof that the stream
of his thought and experience has flowed down
through auriferous soil. "We sail on his memory into
the ports of every nation," says Mr. Emerson admirably in his Introduction to Goodwin's Plutarch's
"Morals." No doubt we are becalmed pretty often,
and yet our old skipper almost reconciles us with our
dreary isolation, so well can he beguile the time,
when he chooses, with anecdote and quotation.

It would hardly be extravagant to say that this delightful old proser, in whom his native Bœotia is only
too apparent at times, and whose mind, in some respects, was strictly provincial, had been more opera-
tive (if we take the "Lives" and the "Morals" together) in the thought and action of men than any
other single author, ancient or modern. And on the
whole it must be allowed that his influence has been
altogether good, has insensibly enlarged and humanized his readers, winning them over to benevolence,
moderation, and magnanimity. And so wide was his

own curiosity that they must be few who shall not find somewhat to their purpose in his discursive pages. For he was equally at home among men and ideas, open-eared to the one and open-minded to the other. His influence, too, it must be remembered, begins earlier than that of any other ancient author except Æsop. To boys he has always been the Robinson Crusoe of classic antiquity, making what had hitherto seemed a remote island sequestered from them by a trackless flood of years, living and real. Those obscure solitudes which their imagination had peopled with spectral equestrian statues, are rescued by the sound of his cheery voice as part of the familiar and daylight world. We suspect that Agesilaus on his hobby-horse first humanized antiquity for most of us. Here was the human footprint which persuaded us that the past was inhabited by creatures like ourselves.

A PLEA FOR FREEDOM FROM SPEECH
AND FIGURES OF SPEECH-MAKERS

A PLEA FOR FREEDOM FROM SPEECH AND FIGURES OF SPEECH-MAKERS

I MUST beg allowance to use the first person singular. I cannot, like old Weller, spell myself with a We. Ours is, I believe, the only language that has shown so much sense of the worth of the individual (to himself) as to erect the first personal pronoun into a kind of votive column to the dignity of human nature. Other tongues have, or pretend, a greater modesty.

I

What a noble letter it is! In it every reader sees himself as in a glass. As for me, without my I's, I should be as poorly off as the great mole of Hadrian, which, being the biggest, must be also, by parity of reason, the blindest in the world. When I was in college, I confess I always liked those passages best in the choruses of the Greek drama which were well sprinkled with *ai ai*, they were so grandly simple. The force of great men is generally to be found in their intense individuality, — in other words, it is all in their I. The merit of this essay will be similar.

What I was going to say is this.

My mind has been much exercised of late on the subject of two epidemics, which, showing themselves formerly in a few sporadic cases, have begun to set in with the violence of the cattle-disease: I mean Eloquence and Statuary. They threaten to render the country unfit for human habitation, except by the Deaf and Blind. We had hitherto got on very well in Chesumpscot, having caught a trick of silence, perhaps from the fish which we cured, *more medicorum*, by laying them out. But this summer some misguided young men among us got up a lecture-association. Of course it led to a general quarrel; for every pastor in the town wished to have the censorship of the list of lecturers. A certain number of the original projectors, however, took the matter wholly into their own hands, raised a subscription to pay expenses, and resolved to call their lectures "The Universal Brotherhood Course," — for no other reason, that I can divine, but that they had set the whole village by the ears. They invited that distinguished young apostle of Reform, Mr. Philip Vandal, to deliver the opening lecture. He has just done so, and, from what I have heard about his discourse, it would have been fitter as the introductory to a nunnery of Kilkenny cats than to anything like universal brotherhood. He opened our lyceum as if it had been an oyster, without any regard for the feelings of those inside. He pitched into the world in general, and all his neighbors past and present in particular. Even the babe unborn did not escape some unsavory epithets in the way of vaticination. I sat down, meaning to write you an essay on "The Right of Private Judgment as distinguished from the Right of Public Vituperation"; but I forbear. It may be that I do not understand the nature of philanthropy.

Why, here is Philip Vandal, for example. He loves his kind so much that he has not a word softer than a brickbat for a single mother's son of them. He goes about to save them by proving that not one of them is worth damning. And he does it all from the point of view of an early (*a knurly*) Christian. Let me illustrate. I was sauntering along Broadway once, and was attracted by a bird-fancier's shop. I like dealers in out-of-the-way things, — traders in bigotry and virtue are too common, — and so I went in. The gem of the collection was a terrier, — a perfect beauty, uglier than philanthropy itself, and hairier, as a Cockney would say, than the 'ole British hairystocracy. "A'n't he a stunner?" said my disrespectable friend, the master of the shop. "Ah, you should see him worry a rat! He does it like a puffic Christian!" Since then, the world has been divided for me into Christians and *perfect* Christians; and I find so many of the latter species in proportion to the former, that I begin to pity the rats. They (the rats) have at least one virtue, — they are not eloquent.

It is, I think, a universally recognized truth of natural history, that a young lady is sure to fall in love with a young man for whom she feels at first an unconquerable aversion; and it must be on the same principle that the first symptoms of love for our neighbor almost always manifest themselves in a violent disgust at the world in general, on the part of the apostles of that gospel. They give every token of hating their neighbors consumedly; *argal*, they are going to be madly enamored of them. Or, perhaps, this is the manner in which Universal Brotherhood shows itself in people who wilfully subject themselves to infection as a prophylactic. In the natural way we might find the disease inconvenient and even expensive; but thus vaccinated with virus from the udders (whatever they may be) that yield the (butter-)milk of human kindness, the inconvenience is slight, and we are able still to go about our ordinary business of detesting our brethren as usual. It only shows that the milder type of the disease has penetrated the system, which will thus be enabled to out-Jenneral its more dangerous congener. Before long we shall have physicians of our ailing social system writing to the "Weekly Brandreth's Pill" somewhat on this wise: — "I have a very marked and hopeful case in Pequawgus Four Corners. Miss Hepzibah Tarbell, daughter of that archenemy of his kind, Deacon Joash T., attended only one of my lectures. In a day or two the symptoms of eruption were most encouraging. She has already quarrelled with all her family, — accusing her father of bigamy, her uncle Benoni

of polytheism, her brother Zeno C. of aneurism, and
her sister Eudoxy Trithemia of the variation of the
magnetic needle. If ever hopes of seeing a perfect case
of Primitive Christian were well-founded, I think we
may entertain them now."

What I chiefly object to in the general-denuncia-
tion sort of reformers is that they make no allowance
for character and temperament. They wish to repeal
universal laws, and to patch our natural skins for us,
as if they always wanted mending. That while they
talk so much of the godlike nature of man, they
should so forget the human natures of men! The
Flathead Indian squeezes the child's skull between
two boards till it shapes itself into a kind of gambrel
roof against the rain, — the readiest way, perhaps, of
uniforming a tribe that wear no clothes. But does he
alter the inside of the head? Not a hair's-breadth.
You remember the striking old gnomic poem that
tells how Aaron, in a moment of fanatical zeal against
that member by which mankind are so readily led
into mischief, proposes a rhinotomic sacrifice to
Moses? What is the answer of the experienced law-
giver?

> Says Moses to Aaron,
> " 'T is the fashion to wear 'em!' "

Shall we advise the Tadpole to get his tail cut off, as
a badge of the reptile nature in him, and to achieve
the higher sphere of the Croakers at a single hop?

A PLEA FOR FREEDOM FROM SPEECH

Why, it is all he steers by; without it, he would be as helpless as a compass under the flare of Northern Lights; and he no doubt regards it as a mark of blood, the proof of his kinship with the preadamite family of the Saurians. Shall we send missionaries to the Bear to warn him against raw chestnuts, because they are sometimes so discomforting to our human intestines, which are so like his own? One sermon from the colic were worth the whole American Board.

Moreover, as an author, I protest in the name of universal Grub Street against a unanimity in goodness. Not to mention that a Quaker world, all faded out to an autumnal drab, would be a little tedious, — what should we do for the villain of our tragedy or novel? No rascals, no literature. You have your choice. Were we weak enough to consent to a sudden homogeneousness in virtue, many industrious persons would be thrown out of employment. The wife and mother, for example, with as indeterminate a number of children as the Martyr Rogers, who visits me monthly, — what claim would she have upon me, were not her husband forever taking to drink, or the penitentiary, or Spiritualism? The pusillanimous lapse of her lord into morality would not only take the very ground of her invention from under her feet, but would rob her and him of an income that sustains them both in blissful independence of the curse of Adam. But do not let us be disheartened. Nature is strong; she is persistent; she completes her syllogism after we have long been feeding the roots of her grasses, and has her own way in spite of us. Some ancestral Cromwellian trooper leaps to life again in Nathaniel Greene, and makes a general of him, to confute five generations of Broadbrims. The Puritans were good in their way, and we enjoy them highly as a preterite phenomenon; but they were *not* good at cakes and ale, and that is one reason why they are a preterite phenomenon.

I suppose we are all willing to let a public censor like P. V. run amuck whenever he likes, — so it be not down our street. I confess to a good deal of tolerance in this respect, and, when I live in No. 21, have plenty of stoicism to spare for the griefs of the dwellers in No. 23. Indeed, I agreed with our young Cato heartily in what he said about Statues. We must have an Act for the Suppression, either of Great Men, or else of Sculptors. I have not quite made up my mind which are the greater nuisances; but I am sure of this, that there are too many of both. They used to be *rare* (to use a Yankeeism omitted by Bartlett), but nowadays they are overdone. I am half inclined to think that the sculptors club together to write folks up during their lives in the newspapers, quieting their consciences with the hope of some day making them look so mean in bronze or marble as to make all square again. Or do we really

[213]

have so many? Can't they help growing twelve feet high in this new soil, any more than our maize? I suspect that Posterity will not thank us for the hereditary disease of Carrara we are entailing on him, and will try some heroic remedy, perhaps lithotripsy.

Nor was I troubled by what Mr. Vandal said about the late Benjamin Webster. I am not a Boston man, and have, therefore, the privilege of thinking for myself. Nor do I object to his claiming for women the right to make books and pictures and (shall I say it?) statues, — only this last becomes a grave matter, if we are to have statues of all the great women, too! To be sure, there will not be the trousers-difficulty, — at least, not at present; what we may come to is none of my affair. I even go beyond him in my opinions on what is called the Woman Question. In the gift of speech, they have always had the advantage of us; and though the jealousy of the other sex have deprived us of the orations of Xantippe, yet even Demosthenes does not seem to have produced greater effects, if we may take the word of Socrates for it, — as I, for one, very gladly do.

No, — what I complain of is not the lecturer's opinions, but the eloquence with which he expressed them. He does not like statues better than I do; but is it possible that he fails to see that the one nuisance leads directly to the other, and that we set up three images of Talkers for one to any kind of man who was useful in his generation? Let him beware, or he will himself be petrified after death. Boston seems to be specially unfortunate. She has more statues and more speakers than any other city on this continent. I have with my own eyes seen a book called "The Hundred Boston Orators." This would seem to give her a fairer title to be called the *tire* than the *hub* of creation. What with the speeches of her great men while they are alive, and those of her surviving great men about those aforesaid after they are dead, and those we look forward to from her *ditto ditto* yet to be upon her *ditto ditto* now in being, and those of her paulopost *ditto ditto* upon her *ditto ditto* yet to be, and those — But I am getting into the house that Jack built.

And yet I remember once visiting the Massachusetts State House and being struck with the Pythagorean fish hung on high in the Representatives' Chamber, the emblem of a silence too sacred, as would seem, to be observed except on Sundays. Eloquent Philip Vandal, I appeal to you as a man and a brother, let us two form (not an Antediluvian, for there are plenty, but) an Antidiluvian Society against the flood of milk-and-water that threatens the land. Let us adopt as our creed these two propositions: —

I. *Tongues were given us to be held.*

II. *Dumbness sets the brute below the man: Silence elevates the man above the brute.*

Every one of those hundred orators is to me a more fearful thought than that of a hundred men gathering samphire. And when we take into account how large a portion of them (if the present mania hold) are likely to be commemorated in stone or some even more durable material, the conception is positively stunning.

Let us settle all scores by subscribing to a colossal statue of the late Town Crier in bell-metal, with the inscription, "VOX ET PRÆTEREA NIHIL," as a comprehensive tribute to oratorical powers in general. *He*, at least, never betrayed his clients. As it is, there is no end to it. We are to set up Horatius Vir in effigy for inventing the Normal Schoolmaster, and by and by we shall be called on to do the same ill-turn for Elihu Mulciber for getting uselessly learned (as if any man had ideas enough for twenty languages!) without any schoolmaster at all. We are the victims of a droll antithesis. Daniel would not give in to Nebuchadnezzar's taste in statuary, and we are called on to fall down and worship an image of Daniel which the Assyrian monarch would have gone to grass again sooner than have it in his back-parlor. I do not think lions are agreeable, especially the shaved-poodle variety one is so apt to encounter; — I met one once at an evening party. But I would be thrown into a den of them rather than sleep in the same room with that statue. Posterity will think we cut pretty figures indeed in the monumental line! Perhaps there is a gleam of hope and a symptom of convalescence in the fact that the Prince of Wales, during his late visit, got off without a single speech. The cheerful hospitalities of Mount Auburn were offered to him, as to all distinguished strangers, but nothing more melancholy. In his case I doubt the expediency of the omission. Had we set a score or two of orators on him and his suite, it would have given them a more intimidating notion of the offensive powers of the country than West Point and all the Navy Yards put together.

In the name of our common humanity, consider, too, what shifts our friends in the sculpin line (as we should call them in Chesumpscot) are put to for originality of design, and what the country has to pay for it. The Clark Mills (that turns out equestrian statues as the Stark Mills do calico-patterns) has pocketed fifty thousand dollars for making a very dead bronze horse stand on his hind legs. For twenty-five cents I have seen a man at the circus do something more wonderful, — make a very living bay horse dance a redowa round the amphitheatre on his (it occurs to me that *hind legs* is indelicate) posterior extremities to the wayward music of an out-of-town (*Scoticè*, out-o'-toon) band. Now, I will make a handsome offer to the public. I propose for twenty-five thousand dollars to suppress my design for an equestrian statue of a distinguished general officer as he *would have* appeared at the Battle of Buena Vista. This monument is intended as a weathercock to crown the new dome of the Capitol at ashington. By this happy contrivance, the horse will be freed from the degrading necessity of touching the earth at all, — thus distancing Mr. Mills by two feet in the race for originality. The pivot is to be placed so far behind the middle of the horse, that the statue, like its original, will always indicate which way the wind blows by going along with it. The inferior animal I have resolved to model from a spirited saw-horse in my own collection. In this way I shall combine two striking advantages. The advocates of the Ideal in Art cannot fail to be pleased with a charger which embodies, as it were, merely the abstract notion or quality, Horse, and the attention of the spectator will not be distracted from the principal figure. The material to be pure brass. I have also in progress an allegorical group commemorative of Governor Wise. This, like-Wise, represents only a potentiality. I have chosen, as worthy of commemoration, the moment when and the method by which the Governor meant to seize the Treasury at Washington. His Excellency is modelled in the act of making one of his speeches. Before him a despairing reporter kills himself by falling on his own steel pen; a broken telegraph wire hints at the weight of the thoughts to which it has found itself inadequate; while the Army and Navy of the United States are conjointly typified in a horse-marine who flies headlong with his hands pressed convulsively over his ears. I think I shall be able to have this ready for exhibition by the time Mr. Wise is nominated for the Presidency, — certainly before he is elected. The material to be plaster, made of the shells of those oysters with which Virginia shall have paid her public debt. It may be objected, that plaster is not durable enough for verisimilitude, since bronze itself could hardly be expected to outlast one of the Governor's speeches. But it must be remembered that his mere effigy cannot, like its prototype, have the pleasure of hearing itself talk; so that to the mind of the spectator the oratorical despotism is tempered with some reasonable hope of silence. This design, also, is intended only *in terrorem*, and will be suppressed for an adequate consideration.

I find one comfort, however, in the very hideousness of our statues. The fear of what the sculptors will do for them after they are gone may deter those who are careful of their memories from talking themselves into greatness. It is plain that Mr. Caleb Cushing has begun to feel a wholesome dread of this posthumous retribution. I cannot in any other way account for that nightmare of the solitary horseman on the edge of the horizon, in his Hartford Speech.

His imagination is infected with the terrible consciousness, that Mr. Mills, as the younger man, will, in the course of Nature, survive him, and will be left loose to seek new victims of his nefarious designs. Formerly the punishment of the wooden horse was a degradation inflicted on private soldiers only; but Mr. Mills (whose genius could make even Pegasus look wooden, in whatever material) flies at higher game, and will be content with nothing short of a general.

Mr. Cushing advises extreme measures. He counsels us to sell our real estate and stocks, and to leave a country where no man's reputation with posterity is safe, being merely as clay in the hands of the sculptor. To a mind undisturbed by the terror natural in one whose military reputation insures his cutting and running (I mean, of course, in marble and bronze), the question becomes an interesting one, — To whom, in case of a general exodus, shall we sell? The statues will have the land all to themselves, — until the Aztecs, perhaps, repeopling their ancient heritage, shall pay divine honors to these images, whose ugliness will revive the traditions of the classic period of Mexican Art. For my own part, I never look at one of them now without thinking of at least one human sacrifice.

I doubt the feasibility of Mr. Cushing's proposal, and yet something ought to be done. We must put

up with what we have already, I suppose, and let
Mr. Webster stand threatening to blow us all up
with his pistol pointed at the elongated keg of gun-
powder on which his left hand rests, — no bad type
of the great man's state of mind after the nomination
of General Taylor, or of what a country member
would call a penal statue. But do we reflect that
Vermont is half marble, and that Lake Superior
can send us bronze enough for regiments of statues?
I go back to my first plan of a prohibitory enactment.
I had even gone so far as to make a rough draught
of an Act for the Better Observance of the Second
Commandment; but it occurred to me that con-
victions under it would be doubtful, from the difficulty of satisfying a jury that our graven images did
really present a likeness to any of the objects enumer-
ated in the divine ordinance. Perhaps a double-
barrelled statute might be contrived that would
meet both the oratorical and the monumental difficulty. Let a law be passed that all speeches delivered more for the benefit of the orator than that of
the audience, and all eulogistic ones of whatever
description, be pronounced in the chapel of the Deaf
and Dumb asylum, and all statues be set up within
the grounds of the Institution for the Blind. Let the
penalty for infringement in the one case be to read
the last President's Message, and in the other to look
at the Webster statue one hour a day, for a term not

so long as to violate the spirit of the law forbidding cruel and unusual punishments.

Perhaps it is too much to expect of our legislators that they should pass so self-denying an ordinance. They might, perhaps, make all oratory but their own penal, and then (who knows?) the reports of their debates might be read by the few unhappy persons who were demoniacally possessed by a passion for that kind of thing, as girls are sometimes said to be by an appetite for slate pencils. *Vita brevis, lingua longa.* I protest that among lawgivers I respect Numa, who declared, that, of all the Camenæ, Tacita was most worthy of reverence. The ancient Greeks also (though they left too much oratory behind them) had some good notions, especially if we consider that they had not, like modern Europe, the advantage of communication with America. Now the Greeks had a Muse of Beginning, and the wonder is, considering how easy it is to talk and how hard to say anything, that they did not hit upon that other and more excellent Muse of Leaving-off. The Spartans, I suspect, found her out and kept her selfishly to themselves. She were indeed a goddess to be worshipped, a true Sister of Charity among that loquacious sisterhood!

Endlessness is the order of the day. I ask you to compare Plutarch's lives of demigods and heroes with our modern biographies of deminoughts and zeroes. Those will appear but tailors and ninth-parts of men in comparison with these, every one of whom would seem to have had nine lives, like a cat, to justify such prolixity. Yet the evils of print are as dust in the balance to those of speech.

We were doing very well in Chesumpscot, but the Lyceum has ruined all. There are now two debating clubs, seminaries of multiloquence. A few of us old-fashioned fellows have got up an opposition club and called it "The Jolly Oysters." No member is allowed to open his mouth except at high-tide by the calendar. We have biennial festivals on the evening of election day, when the constituency avenges itself in some small measure on its Representative elect by sending a baker's dozen of orators to congratulate him.

But I am falling into the very vice I condemn, — like Carlyle, who has talked a quarter of a century in praise of holding your tongue. And yet something should be done about it. Even when we get one orator safely underground, there are ten to pronounce his eulogy, and twenty to do it over again when the meeting is held about the inevitable statue. I go to listen: we all go: we are under a spell. 'T is true, I find a casual refuge in sleep; for Drummond of Hawthornden was wrong when he called Sleep the child of Silence. Speech begets her as often. But there is no sure refuge save in Death; and when my life is

[223]

closed untimely, let there be written on my head-stone, with impartial application to these Black Brunswickers mounted on the high horse of oratory and to our equestrian statues, —

Os sublime did it!

THE END